BUTTERFLIES
OF THE NIGHT

BUTTERFLIES OF THE NIGHT

Mama-sans, Geisha, Strippers,
and the Japanese Men They Serve

LISA LOUIS

NEW YORK • TENGU BOOKS • TOKYO

First edition, 1992

Some of the material in Chapters 2, 3, and 6 appeared originally
in "Elusive, Illusive Gion" (*Winds* magazine, October 1986; in "Reflections of a
Newborn Mama" (*Kansai Time Out*, December 1985); and in "Women of the
Mizu Shobai" (*Kyoto Journal*, Summer 1987). Some of the material in Chapter 7
appeared in "From Exports to Imports: Japan's Trade in Women," (*EastWest
Magazine*, Summer 1987); and in "The *Japayuki-san* Explosion" (*Kansai Time
Out*, March 1987). Some of the material in Chapter 8 appeared in "Mr. S"
(*Kyoto Journal*, Summer 1987).

TENGU BOOKS are published by
Weatherhill, Inc.
420 Madison Avenue, 15th Floor
New York, New York 10017

Library of Congress Cataloging in Publication Data
    Louis, Lisa, 1961–
      Butterflies of the night : mama-sans, geisha, strippers, and the
    Japanese men they serve / by Lisa Louis.—1st ed.
        p.   cm.
    ISBN (invalid) 0-08-348024-9 : $19.95
      1. Hotels, taverns, etc. —Japan—Kyoto. 2. Entertaining—Japan
    —Kyoto. 3. Cocktail servers—Japan—Kyoto. 4. Geishas—Japan
    —Kyoto. 5. Kyoto (Japan)—Social life and customs.   I. Title.
    GT3415.J3L68 1992
    952'. 1864048—dc20   91-45477
                                            CIP

ISBN 0-8348-0249-X

Printed in the U.S.A.

CONTENTS

AUTHOR'S NOTE

All names of people and entertainment establishments have been changed except for purely historical references. Because of the large number of people who have had similar experiences in the *mizu shobai*, it would be quite easy to mistakenly identify one of the interviewees for someone with a seemingly identical story, but similarities to known people are safer considered to be coincidental.

All interviews with Japanese were conducted in Japanese and translated by the author. The word "girl" appears more frequently than the word "woman" in many of the Japanese interviews. This is usually a translation of *onna no ko*, the term for girl, also a diminutive phrase for women.

The opinions expressed by the interviewees do not necessarily reflect the views of the author.

ACKNOWLEDGMENTS

I would like to thank all of the people who gave me information and support during the years *Butterflies of the Night* was being researched and created, particularly the many people who arranged for and gave interviews for the book. Though these people deserve the most thanks of all, I will refrain from naming names here due to the nature of the material and how the entertainment business is viewed in Japanese society.

On the publishing, editing, and research end, thanks go to Cherie Fehrman for helping me get my feet on the ground with the publishing business at the very beginning, to Ed Hardy, Fran Passalacqua, Sherry Fowler, Dale Slusser, and many other friends for keeping their eyes peeled for new research material, and to Roger Campbell for his editorial support. The suggestions and editorial assistance of Jeff Hunter and Liz Preston of Weatherhill are greatly appreciated. I am of course greatly indebted to my literary agent Pamela Pasti for her continuous efforts and ideas. The book would also not have been possible without the unending patience and support of my husband, Hitoshi Shigeta.

To all of you whom I cannot name, to my *mama-sans*, fellow hostesses who became friends, subsidizers of expensive nightclub excursions, and all of you who opened up and talked about a closed world, thank you for sharing with me another side of reality in Japan, but most of all, thank you for your friendship and kindness.

BUTTERFLIES
OF THE NIGHT

Chapter One

JOB HUNTING
IN THE WATER TRADE

 Chandeliers, a grand piano, velvet sofas, and sparkling chrome and glass tables glitter in a room already shimmering with a festive air. Swirls of color blur the room as women fluttering in silks and flowing chiffons dance with their partners: men with money, men with influence, the elite of Japan. This is one of the most exclusive clubs in one of the most exclusive entertainment districts in Japan, Kyoto's Gion. Each night at dusk the narrow streets of the district fill with women in bright colors flurrying to work at the clubs and bars. Thousands of these "butterflies of the night" sweep across Japan's countless entertainment districts, just as they have done for hundreds of years.

Ruling over this glittering scene at the Club Regent is one woman, older than the others, but still exuding the charm of youth when she chooses. In her traditional finery—a kimono and an obi sash that together cost more than three times the average businessman's annual salary—and sitting high on her throne, superior for having survived in Japan's cutthroat club world for over twenty years, the mama-san of Club Regent oversees her hostesses and customers with the eyes of a falcon. She didn't make it this far just by being obsequious to her guests; she got here by working hard and by hardening her heart.

She works in Japan's entertainment industry, the *mizu shobai*, or "water trade," so called because the flow of customers at bars, nightclubs, and restaurants is like water from a tap, sometimes dry, sometimes running full blast. In the *mizu shobai*, women create a deliciously comfortable and ego-boosting world for their male customers. When I was twenty-two, this world became my world. I found myself sitting in those velvet sofas, smiling at those elite Japanese businessmen, pouring their drinks, and lighting their cigarettes.

I forced myself to work late nights and surrendered my mornings to sleep. A non-smoker and light drinker, I spent hours in billows of cigarette smoke and started a new glass of whiskey with each new set of customers. Subservience was a skill that I later realized is one of the greatest profit-making resources in the greatest profit-making machine, Japan.

CONNECTIONS

I had come to Japan straight out of college looking for a chance to learn a new language and culture before starting a climb on some career ladder in the States. I arrived with a tourist visa and found a teaching job, the same pattern that thousands of Western would-be adventurers before me had followed. I signed a contract with a language school, which issued a working visa for me and promised me a moderate but livable salary for the next year. Since it was necessary to have my visa papers processed in a consulate outside of Japan, I made the first of two trips to Busan, Korea, and returned to Japan.

The head of the language school asked me to teach a short intensive class, even though my visa papers were not yet completed; he said that all foreigners worked before their papers came through, and assured me that I didn't need to worry about it. I taught the class, and then went back to Busan to pick up my visa.

Having used up most of my savings on the two trips to Korea, I came back to find that the head of the language school had talked with his accountant and decided that the school had to cut corners somewhere—specifically, in the salaries of his two main teachers. I protested that we had a signed contract, that the immigration officers had processed my visa based on that agreement. He argued that I had worked without the proper papers and would get into trouble if I pressed the issue, and assured me that he was in a position to be more convincing with the authorities than I was. I knew that all the schools had just finished hiring, and that if I wanted to stay in Japan at all, I would have to stick it out at this place until the next semester, when I could move to another school.

Six months passed and I found a job at a different language school, this one run by an American couple that seemed sympathetic to my horror story about the last boss and his lack of regard for contracts. Within the first month, however, I realized that not only was this couple not going to give me the working hours I'd been promised, but they also didn't pay on time. I waited for more than two weeks past payday to get the little bit of money they did owe me.

I was already without much of a reserve fund, and it got to the point where I would cry myself to sleep wondering how I was going to pay my rent, my college loan, and still be able to eat. I had heard other Western women talking about jobs as hostesses, the usual description being that they were paid the equivalent of a hundred dollars an evening for doing nothing but pouring drinks and making conversation. Not only would a job like that help my finances, but it also seemed as if working as a hostess could be the international adventure I was seeking.

My Australian housemates Penny and Julie had been working in some of the hostess clubs of Kyoto's Gion for a couple of months already. Penny, a kind, curvaceous blonde, and Julie, a heavy but attractive brunette, both seemed to manage the job without too much trouble. Knowing that my financial situation was dire, they urged me to try hostessing until I found a better position.

"Go down and talk with the manager at Tres Belle on Sanjo. You're sure to get in with your Japanese," Penny said.

"Make sure to ask for the manager when you get to the door," Julie warned. "Don't let the guys at the front push you around."

The next night, out of my closet came my only pair of high heels. A rust-colored sweater dress helped me play up my very un-Japanese curves. I used makeup to make my already pale skin even whiter (whiteness is a sign of great beauty in the Orient), and pulled my chestnut hair up to one side with a sparkling clasp. This outfit wasn't particularly comfortable for one used to blue jeans and sweaters. Since it was January, a bitterly cold month in Kyoto, I topped everything off with a trench coat, pink mohair scarf, and gloves.

I made my way downtown to Tres Belle, an oasis of light on a surprisingly dark street. Life-size ceramic leopards guarded the red-carpeted entrance way, and circular glass doors glided open as I entered. This was gaudy as only Japan knows how to do gaudy.

Young men in tuxedoes asked me my business; I politely asked to see the manager. While I waited, I caught a glimpse of glittering sequins. Women not only poured drinks here, they also put on a floor show. Men soaked up the atmosphere while figures in white sequin gowns catered to their needs. On stage was a singer in a sparkling black dress with feathery trim. I watched, trying to imagine myself as a waitress in white sequins, when a voice brought me back to reality.

"Come this way." I followed the back of a black tuxedo through what seemed like a door appearing from nowhere. Suddenly we left the world of flashy glamour, up rickety wooden steps to a dimly lit hallway. Through the darkness I could make out doorways on either side. As we went by, yellow lights revealed overweight, tired-looking women putting on false eyelashes and stuffing themselves into tight dresses. The women who caught my eye acknowledged me with threatening scowls.

The corridor ended, and I found myself in a hazy colorless room, standing before a thin, middle-aged man in wire-rim glasses. My tuxedoed guide had disappeared. The man before me knew my purpose before I had a chance to say anything, but I told him why I was there anyway. "Let me see your passport," he said as he looked me up and down. "You speak Japanese pretty well, don't you?" I replied in the humble manner expected; his attitude made me hopeful.

"Ah, too bad. With this visa you can't work here. I'll tell you straight. We're a big club, and we get checked out by the authorities pretty often. Go to the smaller clubs around, there'll be something for you. Immigration doesn't usually bother the smaller places, there are too many of them." My heart sank, but I thanked him for his time and advice. He'd at least been kind enough to make a suggestion. Somehow I felt as if he really understood my predicament. As I turned to leave, I felt his hand pat me on the rear. I could almost hear the smirk on his face as he said goodbye, but I didn't turn around, I just walked straight out the door.

Julie and Penny suggested that I talk to a Dutch woman named Gerta, who had worked at clubs for years. She would know of places for me to try. The next afternoon, we trudged through the slush to an old Kyoto-style wooden house. It took some time for my eyes to adjust to the darkness of the entrance way, and Gerta's room was even darker. Perhaps she wasn't in. But no, there was the orange glow and the smell of a kerosene heater. Silently we entered. Julie sat down by a lump of blankets in the middle of the chaotic room.

The lump moved, groaned, and mumbled in an odd mixture of Japanese and heavily accented English. This was Gerta. How was she? How was her husband? "I haven't seen him for days." Gerta was married to a member of a local rock band. The subject of a hostessing job for me came up. Her momentary silence discouraged me, but before long she was talking away as she looked for something to write on.

"I know the mama-san here very well. Tell her that Lana sent you and she'll help you out." Lana? "I never used my real name at the club. A lot of women don't. Here." She drew a tiny map on the inside of a matchbook. "You can tell her I sent you, but if they ask, please don't tell them where I am or what I'm doing." Gerta's last words to me were, "Don't let things get to you; don't take anything to heart at the club. It isn't worth it."

THE INTERVIEW

My heart thumped as I dialed the number of Club Regent; there was a ring, an answer. A male voice told me to wait after I told him that "Lana" suggested I call about work. The next voice was elegant, enchanting,

8

reassuring. This was the mama-san. I was charmed. Yes, thank you, speaking Japanese is no problem. Yes, of course I could come in for an interview tomorrow evening at 7:30. Hooray! There was hope.

This time I dug out a dark skirt with a slit on the side, the same pair of heels, and a thin V-neck Angora sweater. Hair swept to one side, I bundled up to face the cold on the way downtown. The flash of neon lights helped me see the map on the matchbook as I made my way through the busy back streets of Gion. I found the right street, but there were foreboding omens. Half a dozen men stood in as many yards, all acting as hawkers for cheap sex shows and touchy-feely joints, Japanese "pink salons." Maybe Club Regent wasn't the high-class place I'd thought.

I made my way slowly down a narrow pathway, barely wide enough for people to walk in small groups, much less to allow for the constant traffic of delivery bikes and taxis. Each tall narrow building was marked by dozens of brightly lit club names, sometimes showing four or five different bars on a floor. Finally, after much confusion, I found the "Club Regent" sign. A wide spiral stairway encased in glass led the way to the second floor. Stomach fluttering, I made my way up the steps.

At the top was a long hallway lined with dark doors, each marked with a small symbol of a different club. So *this* was the flashy club scene! It seemed so somber and quiet. Passing by the dark doors, I heard music coming from behind each. On the last door, the name "Club Regent" was painted in red. I'd reached my destination.

A rush of color, sound, and movement hit me as I swung open the door. None of the women running about took notice of me; a young man in a black tuxedo cut through the motion and guided me to a stool at the small bar. I told him I'd come to see the mama-san. He said she wasn't there yet and that I was to speak with him. This left me feeling a bit uncomfortable and suspicious after having made an appointment with her by phone, but I had no choice.

He disappeared for a moment, so I looked at my surroundings. There were as yet no customers. Japanese women filled a number of couches, some doing their nails, some fixing their makeup, some drinking coffee, finishing a take-out meal, and almost all of them talking. Unlike the typical Japanese reaction to the presence of any foreigner—stares, pointing fingers, and silly questions—I was simply ignored. This was surely a sign of something, but I wasn't sure exactly what.

The young manager returned and asked me to write down my address and phone number. He asked my age and was astounded that I was only twenty-two. There weren't many women under twenty-five in this club. "And what days are you available for work?" he asked. That was it; I was hired! "We'll see you next Tuesday at 7:30, then. You understand the dress code, don't you?" I was so relieved to have a chance to start working that I gave a quick yes without asking what the rules were; looking around at the other women, it just seemed that I had to do my best to look dressed up. That was easy enough. What mattered was that I had a job.

I spent the next few days in a state of nervous anticipation. I was happy to have a job that would pay well, but I also had a fear of the unknown. I worked my few teaching hours and tried to get mentally prepared for my upcoming hostess debut the rest of the time. No matter how many questions I asked my friends, it was impossible to know what it would really be like to work in a bar. Sitting on a couch drinking and talking sounded so easy, but there had to be more to it than that. I found out very quickly that there was indeed much more to being a hostess than the simple description I'd heard.

FIRST NIGHT

The manager showed me where to put my coat: a tiny cubicle crammed with the personal effects of fifteen other women. Makeup bags and fur coats all threatened to slide off their shelves onto the paper-buried desk where the evening's calculations were made. Sitting on one of the couches with the other women, I tried to hide how shy and uncomfortable I felt. Time waiting for customers was passed with the same activity I'd caught a glimpse of before. Some of the women ventured to ask me questions, and upon realizing that I could speak Japanese, warmed up to me a bit. This relative inactivity lasted for a full hour and a half. It was already nine o'clock and not one customer had appeared. Could this place really support itself with no business? Were we really getting paid for just sitting?

Suddenly the door swung open and the women cried, *Irasshaimase!* ("Welcome!") as a group of middle-aged men in dark-blue business suits made their entrance and were ushered to their seats. The whole staff suddenly came alive. My heart was pounding with a feeling of helplessness; I knew I'd be expected to do something, but what? I observed other hostesses running with trays of glasses, kneeling before the men's table to offer hot towels, and generally making them feel welcome.

Lisa, *onegaishimasu!* ("Lisa, please!") There was my call. I went to receive my orders from the manager. He pointed to an open spot beside a short, rotund, greying businessman whose face was glowing red. The other men looked younger. By the royal treatment this man was getting, I assumed he was a high-ranking executive, if not the president of a company. The other hostesses motioned for me to sit next to him, and introduced me. The younger men all made pleasant greetings, but the round man was too busy trying to hold himself and his glass up to pay any attention to me.

After making small talk with the other hostesses, the men turned their attention to me, not just the new girl in the club, but also the only *gaijin* (foreigner, or literally, "outside person") there. "Where do you come from?" "How long have you been in Japan?" "What was your purpose in coming to Japan?"

The standard set of questions. The work seemed pretty easy so far.

"Do you have a Japanese boyfriend?" "How do you like him in bed?" Things had taken a bad turn. I tried to parry these questions as best I could without acting too offended or offensive. I thought maybe this was a cultural difference in allowable conversation topics.

Things got worse.

Mr. Big Executive finally noticed me, and realized that I was a foreigner. He asked me some questions in pidgin English, then made some comments about me, including crude remarks about my bust size. Trying very hard not to lose my temper, I observed the actions of the other hostesses for hints on how to react, but none of them was undergoing what I was. I had no example to follow.

During my state of confusion, Mr. Executive decided to push things a step further. In an attempt to minimize his embarrassing conversation, I did my best to ignore him and to speak with the other men at the table. It was then that one of the harsh realities of the hostessing business hit me. The fine upstanding company executive beside me had wrapped his hand around one of my breasts. I almost jumped out of my seat in surprise. I looked around for help from the other hostesses, and though they didn't scream or run to my rescue, as I'd hoped they would, they did seem to understand from the look on my face that I wasn't taking the situation well.

They did their best to lure the man's attentions away from me. He was perturbed because I'd said something in anger as I shoved his hands away. "Rude foreign bitch!" was the gist of the message I heard in Japanese. I was ready to fight to the death, but the eyes of the other hostesses caught me. They had their jobs to protect, and they probably helped me keep mine that night by stopping me from telling the man what I thought of him, or worse, giving him a sharp left to the jaw. Their looks told me that I'd already overreacted, and that I'd better stay calm. I steamed in indignation, thinking that if this is what being a hostess meant, I wouldn't be here for long.

Lisa, *onegaishimasu!* Saved, at least temporarily, by a call to another table.

HAUTE COUTURE

This wasn't the end of grabby customers, nor was it the end of my hostessing career. Over time, I learned some of the tricks that more experienced hostesses use to keep customers' hands to themselves without offending them. A well-timed move to get more ice for the drinks or turning to another customer at just the right moment often worked well. With really persistent types, a smile and joke about not being a "bad boy," or holding a man's hand to keep it from wandering proved to be effective techniques. Truly skillful mental manipulation allowed some veterans to avoid ever getting touched at all. They had a way of convincing these men through words and actions that they were on the verge of getting some kind of special pleasure without having to reach for it.

At the same time that I was learning these survival skills, I also learned other essential aspects of being a passable club companion. Physical trials and traumas of the hostessing job set aside, I soon found out that one of the important issues of this business was clothing. For the Japanese woman working at a top-rate club, perhaps half or more of her ample salary goes for clothing, makeup, and accessories. As they say, money attracts money, and shabby-looking women attract only shabby-looking men. A set responsibility of any woman working at a drinking and entertainment institution is to dress according to the standards of her club. Telling the manager at the end of my interview at Club Regent that I understood the dress code had been a mistake.

Each night before my thrice-weekly excursions into Kyoto's nightclub world, I asked my various housemates to check out my outfit. Since they were American, Australian, Canadian, French, English, and Scottish, the taste in clothes was definitely Western. The outfits I chose—and I didn't have much in the line of dressy clothes to choose from—usually got positive comments, but I rarely got compliments from the other hostesses at the club. It seemed to me that with thousands of dollars' worth of clothing floating around the room, my low-budget attempts at being stylish didn't deserve to be commented upon. But it was more than that, I was later to find.

Club Regent's mama-san was about fifty, a woman of substance, both in girth and in financial worth. She was also a woman of pride, though it seemed to me that her show of pride was more a cover for her insecurities. She was at the top of the heap, and still going strong. Though in her earlier days she had probably taken a more hands-on approach to running her club, now she simply made an evening appearance and chatted for a moment at each table of guests. She left the true management of the place to the manager, a young man a bit on the sleazy side. He was her henchman.

"Lisa!" The call came toward the end of an evening when I was just about to go home. It wasn't a call to a new table; the manager led me to the back room. "Mama asked me to tell you that you have to dress up more. You know, things with shiny material. Dressier things."

I tried my best with silk blouses and skirts, but not many more days passed before I got another call to the back room saying I needed to dress up still more. "You know, suits, one-piece dresses. More shiny things."

Shiny things again. I knew I'd knock 'em dead with the low-cut white fluffy sweater with puffy sleeves and lots of sparkly sequins spread across the front that I'd been given as a gift. I'd never before felt I could wear it anyplace; here was a chance to get some use out of it. The night I wore that, the people in my house said I couldn't go wrong. Into the club I went with confidence. Halfway through the evening, Mama made her appearance. As she sat at a table of customers across the way, I saw her signal to the manager. He kneeled beside her; she glanced in my direction as she whispered into his ear. It wasn't long before the manager came to me with another message from Mama: I wasn't to wear that sweater again. Tears of frustration welled up; I felt not only humiliated, but indignant, because I had done my best with what I had.

The next night I asked one of the hostesses to tell me what I was doing wrong. "You mean no one explained the dress code to you? Basically, it's like this. No cotton, no wool, no sweaters of any kind. One-piece dresses and suits are better than skirts and tops of different colors, but sometimes you can get away with those. Anything with shiny, expensive-looking material is better." Hmmm . . . No cotton, no wool, no sweaters of any kind. This was a tough order to fill in the most bitter part of winter, but as the rest of the hostesses suffered, so would I.

It was clear that the Western sense of style and the Japanese sense of style didn't mesh, at least not in this club. Though Japanese designers create some of the most exclusive fashions in the world, this was not what was worn at Club Regent. Some women wore kimono at all times, some on occasion, and some never. Most women wore Western-style dresses, but they were usually outmoded, or looked like something the mother of the bride would wear.

Word got around that I didn't have much of a wardrobe, and before long the hostesses started giving me dresses and outfits they were no longer interested in wearing. A Korean woman who had melded into Japanese society gave me a very fine kimono, and this was my prize. The rest of the clothes I was given ranged from a one-piece polyester dress in Pepto-Bismol pink with brown leopard spots and an elastic waist, to a high-collared peach-colored dress with buttons down the front, an all-over pattern of large lavender and blue flowers, and an accordion-style gathered skirt. Certainly the most bizarre outfit I was ever given was the see-through deep purple shirt-dress with side slits starting at the hips and going down past the knees, black leopard spots, and the even more enticing leopard heads dotted all over the piece. Needless to say, the only time I wore this item was at a costume party.

When I made my entrance to Club Regent and took off my coat to reveal one of these hot little numbers, all eyes turned to me. "Lisa, you look wonderful tonight! Where did you get that dress? . . . Oh, Keiko gave it to you? You're so lucky!" By the time I worked at a second club, I'd developed a system in which I wore the dresses stuffed into a pair of jeans and under a jacket so that I could ride my bike to work. A quick change in the ladies' room and, poof! I was an instant bar hostess. Much as Western friends and I laughed at the clothes, it was through the generosity of those women that I managed to keep the job.

GARGANTUANS

Being different is something any non-Japanese woman in a Japanese nightclub—or any non-Japanese in Japan, for that matter—gets used to quickly. To be treated as a novelty is standard fare; to remain unnoticed is unusual. The clubs hire non-Japanese women for the express purpose of providing customers something exotic, something special. In fact, the experience of being treated like an alien from outer space, or at least of being the center of attention, becomes so familiar to most foreigners in Japan that it takes them a while to get used to not being set apart from others when they return to their own countries. The majority of my time at Club Regent was spent being the token white, the point of cultural interest for the evening. There were rare occasions, however, when I went relatively unnoticed.

It had been one of the club's busy evenings, and I'd been sitting with a particularly rude pair of customers: a Japanese Elvis look-alike who'd been passing gas as entertainment, and his WW II veteran sidekick. When I heard the now familiar Lisa, *onegaishimasu!*, I bowed my goodbyes and took my glass to the counter to exchange it for a new one. The manager pointed me to the new table. A number of couches had been pushed together; there must be a big party coming in. As I was about to make my way to the table, the door swung open. *Irasshaimase!*, we all cried. Through the door came a number of normal-sized people, and also, stooping as they entered, came three mountains of humanity. I was about to have my first experience entertaining sumo wrestlers.

Empty glass in hand, I walked slowly toward the table, which by now was filled. Where was I to sit? As I approached, the two masses of flesh sitting together against the wall made a space between them so that I could just squeeze in. Managing to get past the table and their giant kimono-covered legs (no small obstacles), I lowered myself into the pit between the two bodies. I felt as if I'd been swallowed up. The awkwardness of my position was corrected by perching on the edge of the couch and leaning conspicuously out to accept my drink and greet the customers. A hostess's job is to be seen.

For the first time, someone had upstaged me; now these customers were the novelty item. The usual round of comments, "Oh, a foreigner!" "Can she speak Japanese?" "Isn't she pretty?" or "What a big bust!" never emerged from the mouths of these sculptural masses. Admittedly, I too was excited about sitting next to real sumo wrestlers, and couldn't wait to tell all my friends. I thought this was purely because I was an impressionable foreigner, but looking around, I realized that it wasn't just me. Rather than the customers paying attention to and amusing themselves with the hostesses, the hostesses were all ogling, sitting in awed silence, or gingerly reaching out to touch a sumo's immense belly, quickly drawing hands back and covering their mouths as they giggled in childlike surprise and embarrassment. The sumo wrestlers themselves sat in martial silence, their reaction to being touched similar to that of a cow tired of trying to brush away flies, giving at most an uninterested bat of an eyelash at the source of annoyance.

Only two of the three giants at the table were actually sumo wrestlers; the third was a large, but slightly slimmer man in his forties. Unlike his young counterparts in their tentlike, cotton kimono and their oiled, perfumed, and specially arranged ponytails, this man wore a Western-style business suit and had a standard short haircut. Despite his more normal appearance, however, this man's mannerisms were no less martial than his young charges'. Never uttering a word except for grunted expressions to his fellow visitors, he allowed Kimiko, the hostess on his right, to feed him. He did not play flirtatious games, and never once thanked Kimiko or even acknowledged her existence.

This man's movements had me hypnotized; he was like an isolated slow-motion element in a high-speed film. As Kimiko attempted to feed him from a huge platter of fresh fruit, he grabbed the delicate little fork from her hand and shoved a shimmering, juicy hunk of green melon into his mouth. It was as if she did not exist. He gradually lowered his hand to the plate of fruit, and after a brief, clumsy attempt at stabbing a piece of apple, he dropped the fork and used his hands to cram various pieces of fruit into his cavernous mouth, chewing slowly and noisily, bits of peel and greenery hanging out the sides of his mouth. My mind's eye saw a brontosaurus feeding in the jungle.

As juice dribbled down his chin, Kimiko wiped his face with a wet towel. I knew that I, too, was supposed to be serving in this way, but I was affected by a mixture of fascination and a strange sort of disgust at this creature who seemed to be unaware of anyone's existence but his own. Later, when I asked my hostess friend Akemi whether the wrestlers were famous or not, she said that they were both young, coming-up-in-the-ranks types who would probably make big names for themselves soon. The other man was an ex-wrestler and a famous *oyakata*, a coach in the sumo stables. Next time I watched *Sumo Digest* on TV, which shows just the juicy bits of the best matches of the day, I noticed on the sidelines a big, fortyish man who looked familiar. It was my brontosaurus!

The young wrestler across the table was kept occupied by the hostesses around him, who couldn't stop reaching out to touch his colossal belly. He didn't seem amused, but he didn't get angry, either. He seemed used to being treated like a showpiece and had achieved an almost perfect ability to ignore others. The wrestler on my left was

perhaps less experienced, but he seemed no more interested in inter-
acting with his surrounding admirers. I would get in trouble with Mama
and the manager if they saw that I wasn't making an attempt at
conversation, so I decided to get to work and talk with this man. As
huge as he was, he had a rather gentle young face; the special oil in his
long hair had a sweet, fresh fragrance that was very pleasant, though
very different from other men's cosmetic scents.

I honestly wanted to know some things about his life and what he
had done to become a sumo wrestler, so my conversation wasn't
forced, as it was with so many other customers. When I asked him how
old he was, he replied with one word, "twenty-two," and I promptly
informed him that we were the same age. Wasn't that a coincidence?
"Ugh." Similarities between us didn't seem to entice him into active
discussion. If he were interested in pumping the token *gaijin* for
information, he would have started long ago. Maybe he liked talking
about himself. "When did you start training as a sumo wrestler?" "At
fifteen." "Wow, that's very young. It must have been difficult all these
years." "Ugh."

I turned back to my right and saw that the brontosaurus was still
refraining from speech and was slowly moving his hand back and forth
from the nearly demolished fruit platter to his juice-covered mouth. No
source of conversation here. He reminded me vaguely of some of the
football players I went to school with. I really did want to know some
things firsthand from these guys about the world of sumo, but obtaining
more than a one- or two-syllable response was an impossibility. I sighed
and took a sip of my watered-down Remy and water. All of a sudden,
the table rose *en masse*; everyone said their thank yous, goodbyes, and
come agains, and the mountains moved out of the premises.

GETTING IN DEEPER

Though I certainly didn't feel like a streetwalker during my time as a hostess, I didn't feel like Doris Day, either. The club world is not what anyone could describe as a wholesome, clean-cut environment. One of the most curious things that struck me when I started at the club was the interaction between the hostesses. Rarely was there a night that a number of hostesses didn't partake in what seemed to me to be a very odd activity.

Each night, there was at least half an hour and sometimes up to two hours of free time before any customers arrived. It was during that lull, as the women typically preened, napped, or talked about their latest shopping trips or dinners out, that I noticed women touching each other, not on the shoulder or arm to make a point in conversation, but on the hips and breasts.

Men grabbing women seemed like a normal part of the game at the club already, but women feeling each others' breasts in the middle of a room full of people seemed distinctly peculiar to me. After observing this activity a number of times, I realized that they were comparing themselves. Who was bigger? Who was firmer? The typical comments were, "You have such a great figure," and, "I wish I was as big as you." With monthly cycles, it was, "Feel this. Haven't I grown since last week?"

After weeks of seeing this same pattern repeated, it too started to seem like a normal part of the game. After the Japanese hostesses got used to my presence, they even included me in their comparisons, at least verbally. Differences between Western and Eastern physiques came to the forefront. "How lucky you are to be big busted!" or "You have big hips, don't you?," followed by, "Yes, but she has a very small waist." On one occasion one of the regular feel-and-compare hostesses even cautiously reached out to see if I was really the size I looked. I felt like the sumo wrestler having his belly touched. The breast comparison saga didn't end here, though.

One Friday night just before 8:00, Club Regent was still void of customers. An unusually quiet spell was suddenly disturbed by one of the hostesses as she came in. Satomi was one of the fastest, funniest talkers in the club, and her raspy, colloquial speech made her an entertaining addition to any table. I admired her for her frankness and for her sense of style. Satomi was one of the only women in the club who wore clothes that were truly fashionable, rather than fitting the dictates of club wear. She was absentminded at times and not terribly refined, but she had a way of carrying herself that commanded respect. More important, she had guts, a quality rarely given a chance to be displayed by Japanese women.

Satomi had never paid particular attention to me. She wasn't unfriendly; she simply didn't make a fuss over foreigners. Everyone had been sitting quietly, gazing off into space this evening when Satomi burst in, whizzed in and out of the coat room, into the bathroom for a quick makeup check, and then back out into the room where we all were sitting. Something about the dress I was wearing that night caught her eye, and she decided to make an issue of it. "Why don't you give some of that away to those of us who need it?" she taunted, referring to the usual anatomical area. I laughed lightly at this, knowing that it was said in good humor, though it came out sounding kind of tough.

Sitting on a bar stool smiling over Satomi's inclination to say whatever popped into her head, I suddenly felt two hands reach around from behind me and grab my breasts. Before I had a chance to react, Satomi said in a raspy voice, "Wow, this feels great!" more in admiration than sensual rapture. Everyone turned to look, good-natured smiles revealing that they'd all thought about doing the same thing but had never had the nerve. When she stopped and walked away, I noticed out of the corner of my eye that Tsuji-san, the second-ranking manager and a bit of a clown, was approaching with his hands outstretched to get his chance, too. A loud "Get lost, Tsuji-san!" was all he got out of the affair, to everyone's delight. He slinked away with a look of disappointment, mumbling that it just wasn't fair.

Despite these occasional bizarre experiences, I had gradually started feeling as if I was somehow a part of this world. The benefits of the job—short hours, high pay, accurate and on-schedule payment—were things that I wasn't going to give up easily. I also knew that I was getting a unique education in contemporary Japanese culture.

The drawbacks were also becoming more obvious, though. The Japanese man I'd been dating had cooled since I started working as a hostess. Though he knew I wasn't a sleazy bar type, he had traditional views, and he did his best to discourage me from working, even offering me money to get by. I preferred doing an unpleasant job to borrowing money from anyone, so quitting the club was not in the picture.

Gradually, time spent in the club was more comfortable, and I began to be perceived as a club regular by fellow *mizu shobai* workers. Having people come in from "outside," however, was a different story. One night some Japanese men brought in two Americans—a black man and a white woman—who were in Japan on business. I was sent to their table. It was the first time I had talked with Westerners on club turf. We had a great time chatting about their being here to do lectures, both as experts in their fields (yet all of the Japanese assumed that they must be husband and wife, since no woman would actually be an expert in anything!). The conversation was so natural and enjoyable that I forgot I was working. When I heard the cry of Lisa, *onegaishimasu!* and had to move to another table, I had a jolt of realization. For all practical purposes, I was nothing more than a talking puppet.

My story could be told in slightly different ways by countless other women. The following chapters tell the stories of a variety of women and men that I got to know while working in this phenomenal trade. Japanese hostesses, mamas, and geisha reminisce about what brought them to the business. Americans, Europeans, Australians, Filipinas and other "novelty" hostesses reveal their secret lives as club workers. Customers who frequent the clubs tell about their connections with the *mizu shobai*, and a member of the *yakuza*, Japan's own version of the Mafia, gives his philosophy on what makes this world tick.

My career as a hostess was short by Japanese standards, but long enough to spark an interest in understanding the *mizu shobai*. How did these women feel about their work? What really motivated men to frequent these places? Could the industry survive the social and political changes sweeping the country? This book is the culmination of five years of firsthand interviews, exploration, and research. An outsider in Japan, I had the chance to look at the club world from the inside, and received an education in sociology and Japanese business techniques that no university can match. As strange and remote as the *mizu shobai* world may seem to a Westerner, deep beneath it lie the hearts of people who are motivated by and feel the same things as the rest of us.

Chapter Two

A HIGH-CLASS AFFAIR

 Japan's night butterflies are as diverse as the men they serve: short, tall, fat, thin, young, old, university grads, high school dropouts, those who do, those who don't, pretty, plain, elegant, crass. But despite the diversity of women who choose the *mizu shobai* path, there are also points of common ground—a need or desire for money, perhaps a distaste for sedentary office work, and often a desire to be independent, both socially and financially.

The *mizu shobai* covers a wide range of businesses. In the upper echelon are the high-class hostess bars and nightclubs, the *crème de la crème* of contemporary drinking establishments. These elite establishments dot the entire country, with famous (or infamous) concentrations in Tokyo's Ginza, Osaka's Kita Shinchi, and Kyoto's Gion. The expensive, classy bars cater to high-level executives with big expense accounts, as well as to wealthy men paying their own way. For their money, men are entertained by beautiful women in extravagant surroundings, are served the finest whiskey and most elaborate cuisine, and may be treated to live music. One block of Kyoto's Gion alone houses dozens of these establishments. The mercurial nature of the business makes it impossible to tell at any given time exactly how many high-class clubs exist, but in each of the cities mentioned above, there are hundreds.

Of the thousands of women who entertain at these clubs, each has her own unique story and reasons for being part of the business. During the months that I worked at two clubs, I met many Japanese hostesses. Some of them were very kind, helping me survive in an unfamiliar and often unfriendly environment, while others treated me with derision and made my already shaky stay in the bar world even less pleasant. I spent years researching and interviewing *mizu shobai* workers, but as willing as many women seemed to be interviewed about their *mizu shobai* careers, there were often restraints that prevented truly open exchanges, and my naiveté even after a stint as a hostess led me to a number of situations in which I put interviewees in precarious positions.

I started an interview at a restaurant with a hostess I was well acquainted with by asking how things were with her lover, an older, married man she had been seeing for years. At first she pretended she hadn't heard the question. I repeated the inquiry, intending it as a friendly conversation opener. She caught my eyes with hers and gave a reply that twisted the meaning of my question, making her relationship with the man sound strictly professional rather than personal. She motioned with her eyes to a nearby table, and I realized that sitting there was someone who knew this man, perhaps a coworker. I came close to unintentionally revealing a secret affair that could cause her lover big problems if it were made public.

Before I realized how strongly working in the *mizu shobai* could affect a person's social status, I tracked down a hostess acquaintance who worked during the day in one of Kyoto's large department stores. She seemed happy to see me, and had supposedly been told by another hostess that I was going to approach her for an interview. When I started talking about doing research on the *mizu shobai* for a book and tried to make arrangements for an interview, she looked at me in disbelief, and responded as if she couldn't understand why on earth I was speaking to her about this. It didn't take me long to realize that the other workers within hearing distance didn't know about her hostessing job after store hours. I later found out that many department stores have a rule forbidding their employees to work in the *mizu shobai*, and I was putting this woman's daytime job in jeopardy. She never did give me an interview.

Despite a number of fumbled attempts to obtain interviews, I managed to speak with many club hostesses who were willing to talk about their lives in the *mizu shobai*. The Japanese reputation for being reserved and keeping their cards held from view carried into many of these interviews. Most of the Japanese women were far less candid about their lives than non-Japanese interviewees were. What is not said is in some ways just as revealing an aspect of the culture of Japan and its relationship to the night entertainment industry as what is said. The stories of six high-class hostesses and mamas follow.

TERUKO

"Hostessing was the fastest way to make money. I like to travel and I have expensive hobbies. It was also the only way to support my parents." Thirty-six and single, Teruko lives a two-minute walk from the apartment that she rents for her aging parents. "I started hostessing after graduating, when I was twenty-two. I didn't like the idea of just sitting at a desk; I like moving around. I found my first job listed in a newspaper."

Teruko drives a red sports car and wears fur coats and expensive clothes. She travels frequently to exotic places—to the tropics for scuba diving and to winter resorts for skiing. In comparison, the typical contemporary Japanese woman would have quit her job at twenty-four, married at twenty-five, and been at home with two children by thirty. Not only does Teruko's lifestyle defy the conceivable possibilities of almost any Japanese woman, it is also quite out of reach of most well-paid salarymen.

Teruko recently retired from hostessing, but for years she worked flexible hours, and was frequently taken out to dinner by well-to-do men as a peripheral part of her job. She spent most of her work hours sipping oolong tea, smiling, and saying charming things, and for that she earned more in a month than most young businessmen do in three or four. Teruko was a bar hostess at Club Rouen, one of the most popular high-class clubs in Kyoto's Gion. It seats about fifty people, and has twenty hostesses. Teruko wore her long hair pulled away from her face, managed to get by with much less makeup than most of the women she worked with, and dressed more tastefully than many. She was so adept at handling men in a natural, sincere way that it was hard to tell she was actually working when she was at the club. Contrary to what most Westerners might imagine, Teruko did not sleep with customers, nor was her life really that of a playgirl.

"The most I ever made in one month was ¥850,000 (about $6,800; at the time of writing, one dollar equalled approximately 125 yen), but I averaged about ¥650,000 at Club Rouen. The average hostess probably makes about ¥300,000 a month." A decent monthly salary for a young busi-nessman would be ¥250,000, even after averaging in a hefty annual bonus. At Club Rouen, the hostesses' pay depends on their experience, ability, and the number of customers they bring in. Each hostess has a daily pay rate, on top of which she earns a percentage of sales based on how many of her customers come in. No hostess receives a monthly salary. "I made ¥16,000 a day for working from 7:30 p.m. to 12:30 a.m. Hostesses often call in at the last minute to cancel a night of work, which is why a place like Rouen needs so many. When someone calls in sick, they're never caught short.

"Actually, it's ideal for a club to have half and half: a solid group of long-term hostesses who bring in a regular pool of customers, and short-term girls. Clubs need the stability of long-term hostesses, but they also need the appeal of fresh faces coming in fairly often. Men get tired of seeing the same girls all the time. It's best to have one girl per customer, but when the club gets really crowded, that's not possible. Even at the busiest times, there would be at least one hostess for each table of customers." Club Rouen flies high even when other bars and clubs are in a slump because the mama is very smart about the girls she chooses. Most of them are professional hostesses who brought with them a good number of loyal customers from their last club.

One element of the club system common to almost all elite clubs is reflected in *ichigensan okotowari*, a phrase that literally means "first timers are refused" but translates to "no one gets in without an intro-duction." Club pricing systems vary, and although Rouen is not the most expensive club in Kyoto, it is far from the cheapest. Becoming a club member requires purchasing a bottle of whiskey to be brought out for private use on future visits. Opening a new bottle of ¥2,000 whiskey can cost ten or twenty times that much when it means being part of such a "bottle keep" or member system. According to Teruko, "If a man came in alone and spent a couple of hours at the club, he would probably pay about ¥35,000; ¥80,000 if he spent the whole evening. Rouen's prices are mid-range."

Clubs don't charge exact prices for other beverages and food served; these are all combined into general figures. "It's cheaper when men come in a group. If ten guys came in, they wouldn't each pay ¥35,000; it would be much less than that." Many men are on company expense accounts, so they don't have to worry about the consequences of their habits. "I'd say at Rouen half the men come in privately, and half on business."

The mama of Rouen is a careful, calculating businesswoman. Not only does she keep a balance of regular hostesses and new faces, but she also makes sure she always has one or two Western hostesses to provide exotic appeal. Teruko explains. "Japanese men have a thing for Western women. An American or European girl who can speak only a few words of broken Japanese seems cute and helpless to them. Men like trying to help women like that. A foreigner who speaks fluent Japanese doesn't have the same appeal. She isn't as fun anymore." This comment brought to mind my peremptory dismissal from Club Regent. The management had begun to see my ability to speak Japanese as a drawback, for the very reasons that Teruko mentioned. One evening when I came in to hang up my coat, the manager steered me back around, took me to a coffee shop, and told me I was being replaced. There was a Canadian woman who was willing to work five nights a week instead of my three, and I'd already been there long enough for many of the customers to be used to me. This sort of thing happened to Japanese hostesses all the time, but I had thought being a foreigner would make me immune. I was mistaken.

In discussing the appeal of foreign women in Japan's clubs, Teruko is quick to point out that for Club Rouen's mama, "exotic" means white. "Mama doesn't like hiring Taiwanese or Philippine girls. They're much cheaper to employ, but they also tend to get involved in prostitution. Mama wants to avoid giving the club a low-class image." This is not to say that Mama doesn't allow coarse or vulgar behavior in her club. The customer is always right, and if the customer wants sleazy sex talk, that's what the hostesses give him. "A hostess has to be able to talk about a wide variety of things. If a man likes stiff, formal discussions, she should be able to converse accordingly. If he likes to talk about sex, she should be able to handle that, too."

The minimum legal age for hostessing is eighteen. "A hostess can work up to any age if she can still bring in customers. The oldest hostess at Rouen when I was there was about thirty-nine." This sounds great in theory, but many *mizu shobai* women find that life gets tougher as they get older. A business based on looks, youth, and charm isn't easy on those fighting gray hair, expanding middles, and wrinkles. Mamas can get away with signs of advancing age because they are managing the business rather than simply drawing the customers in. "The mama of Club Rouen has gotten more cold-hearted with age. When she started out, she was selling her own charm. Now that she's up around sixty, she has to sell the charm of the girls she hires. If they don't help the business pick up, they're gone. These days, customers don't go to a club just because the mama is a nice person. You have to run a tight ship to survive."

Hostesses have to follow the rules of the club, both spoken and unspoken. "Hostesses spend a lot of their earnings on clothes and makeup. That's part of the job. They're expected to dress appropriately." Do clubs allow a woman to tell a man to stop touching her if she doesn't like it? "There's no rule like that, but of course it's not good for business if hostesses get angry with customers. They have to find ways to prevent such behavior without upsetting the customer. There are other businesses specifically set up to allow men to touch women, so it's OK to try to keep men under control at a first-rate club." As Teruko spoke, I couldn't help but be reminded of my first night at Club Regent, and my helpless attempts to fight off my aggressive tablemate. If only I had known then the things that women like Teruko taught me later.

Are there rules about drinking? "It's a matter of balance. If a hostess gets flat-out drunk, it doesn't look good, but she's expected to drink with the customer to make him feel good. I can't drink alcohol, so I told the management of Rouen that if they wanted me, they'd have to accept the fact that I don't drink." There are other reasons to drink besides making customers feel comfortable. "Big money comes in every time a customer opens a new bottle. Hostesses are encouraged to drink up when they see a bottle dwindling so that the next bottle will be opened." And what about food? "The food is for the customers, and a girl shouldn't be seen gobbling food down like a pig, but it's the same as the whiskey—if a plate isn't empty, the next dish can't be brought out. Sales go up every time a new plate of food comes out."

Anyone spending even ten minutes in a Japanese hostess bar would assume that some of the women sleep with customers after hours, but again, there are no explicit rules governing the subject. "If a girl sleeps casually with a customer, he'll eventually get tired of her. If he stops seeing her, he'll stop coming to the club, and that's bad for business.

There is no set rule, but doing anything that jeopardizes business is frowned upon."

What about women who do sleep with customers, essentially acting as prostitutes? "I'd say the majority of hostesses have slept with customers for something, though it's not always money. Some girls get fur coats, others get diamonds. Sure, it's tempting to go that route, because it's profitable, but if one has beliefs and sticks to them, that won't happen. I'm talking about very short-term affairs, as opposed to long-term relationships where there's really some feeling between the two. That's different." Teruko speaks from experience: She is the mistress of one of her club customers, and has been for many years.

"I was married once, but I don't have any desire to marry again, and I'm too old to have children. There aren't many men who can handle financially and emotionally independent women." Is the independent type her ideal of what a woman should be? "I like being who I am, but when I see naive, dependent girls, they strike me as being very cute."

Being a *mizu shobai* woman used to carry a very strong social prejudice, and that still remains to some degree. It is difficult for *mizu shobai* women to get married. "Even if the man's parents agree, the rest of the relatives usually make a lot of noise and prevent the marriage. I don't feel sorry for *mizu shobai* women, though. They've chosen that path for themselves. There's nothing hostesses can do about being looked down on by some people. I never felt ashamed about working as a hostess. I used my own name at the club, and all my friends and relatives knew what I did. I felt good about myself. Maybe I was the victim of prejudice sometimes and was too dense to realize it."

Teruko quit her lucrative hostessing career for a much lower-paying job as general assistant at an architectural design firm. Even with the decrease in income, the good points of the new job make it worth the switch. "I liked about seventy percent of hostessing and disliked about thirty percent. I finally just got tired. Your body has to function the complete opposite of everyone else's, getting up at night to work, sleeping in the day. If I really felt I was suited to the *mizu shobai* world, I would have become the mama of my own club. But I never felt a desire to do that. It's just not me.

"If I were a man, I probably wouldn't go to clubs for entertainment. These clubs exist because Japanese are not good at making conversation. In the old days, people of the opposite sex couldn't talk to each other in public easily. Those days are over." Does that mean the *mizu shobai*'s existence is in danger? "In the future, the number of middle-class clubs may decrease, but the very expensive and very cheap places will always do well. Clubs are necessary for conducting business in Japan. Even with the trend toward developing business connections on the golf course instead of in bars, the club business will never die."

SUPREME MAMA

The stark white skin and rich black hair of Club Supreme's mama seem to reflect the winter scenes of her hometown in Japan's snow country. She wears Western clothes, unlike most kimono-clad mamas in Kyoto's bars. Her clothes are striking and attractive, but not overly suggestive or sensuous. She sits primly and speaks with an educated air and a clear sense of confidence.

"I started in this business only seven years ago. I really didn't have any experience in the *mizu shobai*, but jumped right in as a mama. I borrowed money from a bank to start this club. At first my family opposed my choice, but now that I'm taking care of my mother, she doesn't complain." This mama used to be an OL, or "office lady," one of the thousands of underpaid young women who scurry about in offices doing clerical work and making tea. "I studied English at the YMCA after work and then took a trip to the United States to study more." When she came back from the States with her improved English, Mama taught children's classes and gave private lessons.

"It occurred to me that there were probably a lot of people, especially working men, who really wanted to study English but just couldn't drag themselves off to study after a long day at the office. I decided to open a club where men could come in for a beer after work and relax while practicing their English." Mama runs a small club with two Japanese hostesses, one Western hostess, a guitar player, and a waiter. "My Japanese girls are office workers earning extra money by working part-time at night. They aren't hardened, professional hostesses. I like it better that way."

Despite her well-laid plans, the business didn't turn out exactly as she had expected. Having a native English speaker at the club is a drawing factor, but not for all of her clients. "It's good to have a Western girl here for my customers who want to practice their English in a relaxed atmosphere, but many men come here for reasons totally unrelated to that. That's why I have to have both Japanese and Western girls. Having an English speaker is also helpful when Japanese customers bring in foreign clients. The Japanese men are usually exhausted from struggling the whole day to speak English, and when they come to my club, they can leave the talking to the Western hostess."

I had my own interesting language experience one night at Club Regent, when I ended up sitting in the midst of a rowdy group of young businessmen from a lingerie company. I was immediately shoved next to a quiet-looking young Japanese man who seemed sorry for his comrades' behavior. "He speaks English! Speak English!" I'd heard this a million times before. The big thrill of the night was to have the one member of the group who could spew out a few words of English stammer at the foreign hostess. We ignored each other for awhile, not wanting to put on a show for his colleagues. When he actually did speak, I was astounded. He spoke perfect English, with an Australian accent. We spoke at length about his time spent in Australia, and what he was doing back here in Japan. When the subject turned to me, I suddenly felt ashamed. For someone who knew both the Western and the Japanese world to see me as a club hostess was mortifying.

Supreme Mama concedes that having a Westerner as a novelty item seems to be an asset, but "there are problems. Since I have only one foreign girl working each night, if she suddenly decides to take the night off, all the pressure's on me to entertain in English if someone brings in foreign customers." That's not the only problem this mama sees. "Sometimes Japanese treat *gaijin* too well. The women get spoiled and don't do the same work as the Japanese girls; they just sit like a flower arrangement and get paid twice or more what the Japanese do. I do have one Australian girl who works just as hard as the Japanese hostesses. She's worth paying because she can speak Japanese, too. Other foreigners come in having been paid some outrageous wage for doing nothing at another bar and expect to get the same pay automatically. They figure they're owed high wages purely because they are *gaijin*."

The ups and downs in the entertainment industry don't worry the Supreme's mama too much. "There will always be a need for a place where you can conduct business informally. People don't take out just their clients; bosses take out their employees to keep them happy, too."

Keeping customers loyal means keeping business flowing at a reasonable pace. "If a club is completely dead, customers will come only because they feel sorry for the mama. If it's really busy, they won't come because they figure they're not needed. It's important to keep a balance. Having to turn customers away when the club is packed is painful because there are so many other times when we really need them."

Of course there are times when club work isn't pleasant. "There's no such thing as a job that you love to death. Sure, I sometimes want to drop it all and quit, like when there's a conflict with a customer. I don't like men who don't have manners, who don't follow even basic social rules." Not getting paid is another problem. "Having to press for payment makes me feel bad. Guys who can't pay often have some kind of personal problem, or perhaps their company has gone under. Some clubs used to get payment by sending a bill; they wouldn't accept cash at the door. When the man got the bill, it served as a reminder of the club, and when he came in to pay it, it meant he would spend another evening and more money. Nowadays clubs are usually more than happy to accept cash on the spot."

Has it been worth taking the plunge into the *mizu shobai* world? "If I choose to continue being a mama past sixty, I can do it. Having started this place from scratch, I want to keep it going, to make it work. This business has its good points and bad points, but I think I made the right choice."

HITOMI MAMA

Club Hitomi's neon light can be seen from one of the busiest corners of Kyoto's bustling entertainment district, the crossing of Shijo and Hanamikoji streets. It was here that my hostessing education and adventures continued after I left Club Regent. Club Hitomi is much smaller than the Regent, my hours were longer, and the pay wasn't as good, but the atmosphere was cozy, the mama-san was big-hearted, and the manager and *chiifu* ("chief," a rank denoting the man who prepares and organizes the food and drinks) were kind men who took a sincere interest in their hostesses' welfare. There were five hostesses as opposed to the Regent's almost twenty, and I was the first and only foreigner to work there. At Club Hitomi I was exposed to facets of Japan and the *mizu shobai* that I had not yet seen, including the notorious *yakuza*, and I got to know the people at this more intimate club better.

Hitomi's mama is fortyish and sports an Annette Funicello-like hairdo held together with plenty of hairspray. Calling her petite is an understatement, since even with *zoori* sandals on beneath her kimono, she doesn't stand a full five feet. The Japanese saying, *sansho wa kotsubu demo piriri to karai*, or "A pepper is small, but packs a sharp punch," fits this mama well. Behind her warm laugh and infectious smile is a mind that is always working at ways to keep her business rolling.

Like the mama of Club Supreme, the mama of Club Hitomi came from a good family that would never have dreamed that their daughter would enter the *mizu shobai*. Her father worked for the National Railway, and government workers were expected to uphold certain social conventions. "There was still a very strong prejudice against bar and entertainment workers. People thought I was crazy to choose the *mizu shobai* life. I had graduated from a prestigious four-year national university, and it didn't make sense to anyone that I would choose this profession.

"Just out of college, I worked in the office of one of Japan's largest companies. People thought I was crazy to quit that, too. But for a woman, there was no chance to advance in those days. It hasn't changed much even today. At ¥120,000 a month, how was I supposed to support my parents?" Like Teruko, Hitomi's mama is an only child, and she knew that at some point she would have to take care of her mother and father, as Japanese tradition dictates. "I wasn't particularly interested in getting married, and besides, many families don't want their son to marry a woman who's responsible for her own parents. They want a daughter-in-law who's free to take care of them in their old age. I knew I'd have to shoulder the financial responsibility of my parents on my own."

With this heavy financial burden looming, even with the best education and the best job a woman could get, this mama knew it wasn't enough. "In the sixties, the only high-paying option for an independent woman was the *mizu shobai*." But she met with opposition. "My family was in Wakayama, and it would have been a great embarrassment for any relatives in the area to know that I was working in the *mizu shobai*. I decided to go to Kyoto to become a hostess. I was going to work and save money until I was thirty and then buy my own club. My parents opposed the idea, but I went anyway."

Mama arrived in Kyoto and started a successful career as a bar hostess. "After eight years as a hostess, I opened my own club. That was in 1977." Did this career move break off her family relations entirely? "My parents don't complain about my decision now. I built them a house in Kyoto. I hadn't intended to marry, but just before I opened my own place I met someone and we got married. We have a daughter in elementary school."

There are a surprising number of married women among *mizu shobai* workers, though as with anyone else, their marriages aren't always completely successful. "The reason I didn't want to get married was that I thought it would get in the way of business, that I wouldn't be able to devote enough time to running a business and having a husband and family. It isn't easy after all." Mama also admits that her husband has not always been faithful to her. Many Japanese, particularly in Mama's age group, consider it acceptable for a husband to have mistresses but not for a wife to have lovers. "Of course I don't like it, but that's the way things are. I concentrate on other things, like my daughter." For a woman in a business that concentrates on sensual interaction between men and women, Mama seems to take a very traditional view. "Sure, I'd like to have the warmth and closeness of someone special and true, but I'm a married woman, and I chose this husband and this life and have to make the most of them."

Marriage is not always easy, and neither is business. "The last couple of years have been rough. My club is going through a tough spell. I can't let the hostesses know when we're in the red. Even if it comes out of my savings, the girls always get their pay. The average pay at my place is about ¥300,000 a month, but my top earner gets ¥700,000. Things were better for me in the old days. When I was a hostess I often brought home ¥1,200,000 a month. That was great, especially when you consider inflation."

Mama has managed to survive the financial pressures of the business, but what about societal pressures? "There's much less prejudice now than there was twenty years ago. Now being a hostess is just considered another occupation. I'm sure there's still some discrimination, but it's not like the days when a hostess couldn't get married or find any other kind of work." Like Teruko, Mama also doesn't feel much prejudice herself, perhaps due to her own sense of purpose. "I imagine unpleasant incidents must have occurred when I was a hostess, but I ignored whatever prejudice there may have been. I did my work with pride, because I felt I had a future, a goal. I am now the owner and manager of my own business, so people don't look down on me. On top of that, I'm married, have a daughter, and live with my parents. I'm treated with respect. When I leave my daughter to go to work in a kimono and fur stole, the neighbors don't say, 'Poor little girl, her mother works in the *mizu shobai*.' They say, 'Isn't she lucky to have a nice house and expensive things!'"

Society's attitude toward the *mizu shobai* hasn't changed totally, but it has softened. Department-store clerks and office workers work as hostesses at night to make extra money. It is common to find single mothers—women who are divorced, widowed, or were abandoned— working both day and night jobs. It's the only way they can feed their kids and pay the rent.

"Why should such women, who are honestly struggling to support a family, be looked down on? The way society is today, people have no right to put them down. Perfectly 'respectable' women—housewives, college coeds, and the like—are signing up at *aijin banku* [mistress introduction services] just so they can have some play money. They're sleeping with customers for money, whereas a hostess is pouring drinks and making conversation for hers. I'm not saying there are no hostesses who sleep with men for money, but many don't, and if they do, it's separate from club business."

Mama is cheerful, friendly, and warm, unlike the mamas of many clubs. Her honesty and kindness may be part of what puts her club in the red at times. The cold-hearted, shrewd mamas may do better financially, but Hitomi's mama can live knowing that she's been a good person besides keeping her business running. "Rather than say I'm happy or unhappy about my life, I'd have to say that this was the path I had to choose. As far as that choice goes, things seem to have worked out pretty well."

ISHIDA-SAN

People talk about the "old days" of *mizu shobai* even when referring to the 1960s. Going back to the really old days, the war era, offers a whole new perspective on the modern-day *mizu shobai*. In the 1930s and 1940s, entering the nightclub business was a necessity for more women than it is today. One of them, the self-assured and talkative Ishida-san, remembers how the war and the *mizu shobai* changed her life.

Born in 1920, Ishida-san was a teenager when Japan occupied Manchuria. "Dance halls were popular back then. There would be more than a hundred dancers in a big place with two bands, a tango band and a swing band. The dancing girls would stand or sit off to the side and wait for men to select them for a dance. Women wore long dresses or kimono."

Buying power was different in those days. The *sen*, which is worth one hundredth of a yen, still had real value then. "A ticket at the dance hall was about fifteen *sen*, which was good for one song, about three minutes of dancing. A man could give as many tickets as he wanted to one girl. It was good for the dancer, because that boosted her sales and popularity."

A comparison of earnings helps put these outdated prices into perspective. "Dancers could pull in anywhere from ¥200 to ¥300 a month. A Tokyo University graduate [considered the best university in the nation] could earn about ¥70 or ¥80 monthly in the business world." That's the equivalent nowadays of $25,000 a year for the graduate compared to something like $75,000 for a dance-hall girl. "Back in those days people were still selling their children to survive. If you wanted money, you went into the *mizu shobai*." But despite the good money she could have made as a dance-hall girl, Ishida-san chose to stay at home and help her family; she didn't work at any outside jobs, even in her mid-twenties. "Back then the prejudice against *mizu shobai* girls was terrible. A family member of a *mizu shobai* worker couldn't get a government job."

Ishida-san married in her late twenties, and within six months was a war widow. "I opened a coffee shop to make a living. I had done what most people did during the war—moved to the countryside where it was less dangerous." She ran her coffee shop in Yamaguchi Prefecture for twelve years. "I liked cooking and all, but wanted to get out of the countryside. There wasn't much going on there, and there was no new business for a shop." She had an acquaintance in Kyoto who helped her get started at a *sunakku* ("snack," or small bar). "Since there was no bartender, I did almost everything myself. I had three girls working for me. I can't drink alcohol, so it was good to have the girls there to drink with the men."

Kyoto was new territory for Ishida-san. "I'd rented a place on Kiyamachi. I was doing OK with that when someone in the same neighborhood talked me into buying a bar. It was a bad deal and I lost a lot of money. I would have been better off being just a mama and not an owner." Still, Ishida-san claims, the *mizu shobai* is the fastest way to independence. She had to make it on her own when her husband died, which wasn't easy. "Making a profit depends on the way you run your business." This timeless truth may not have changed, but other aspects of the *mizu shobai* have.

"Back then girls didn't switch clubs as often as they do now. Bars gave the girls a percentage of sales based on how much money their customers spent, a system that some clubs still employ. We used to call customers to get them to come to the bar. The *doohan* system, where the hostesses bring the customers in as part of a weekly or monthly quota, is very recent. So is calling bar girls 'hostesses.' Girls who were hired as companions for parties were called 'hostesses' then. Now those girls are called 'companions.'" Western clothing wasn't as popular in those days, and all of Ishida-san's hostesses wore kimono.

Ishida-san has seen many trends and changes over the years. "The *mizu shobai* in general didn't change much with the closing of the *akasen* [Japan's legal red-light districts, which were regulated by the government and closed in 1958], but society did. Men used to have a place to go for sex—society considered it pretty normal for men to hire prostitutes—but now it's not legal. That's why you have more rape and murder these days, why young girls get killed. You never used to see porn magazine vending machines in the old days. I believe it would be better to have something legal so there would be fewer sex crimes and less disease."

Ishida-san didn't stay in the *mizu shobai* all that long. She quit the bar business and studied to earn a certificate as a kimono teacher. Until her recent retirement, she worked in Osaka for many years, teaching young women how to wear and take care of kimono. Ishida-san never remarried—"It would have been a pain in the neck to me," she says. "I like being independent"—and she lives with her sister now. "I have my own space, and I'm never lonely."

OPULENCE MAMA

Some mamas make a go of it, some don't. Clubs open, clubs close. There is a great deal of turnover in mamas as well as hostesses, and people who can make it work long-term and feel they are on top of the business aren't all that plentiful. The mama of Club Opulence has managed to survive for close to twenty years, but she is not all that positive. Her face shows signs of care that makeup can't hide.

"I've run this club for eighteen years now. When I started out in the *mizu shobai*, I spent four or five years working nights in a club, and days at a regular job. When my body couldn't take it anymore, I had to make a decision between the daytime job and the nightclub world. At that time, a day job paid barely enough to cover room and board and one piece of clothing. Since there was no suitable marriage partner around for me at the time, I decided to go for the night work."

This mama saved up enough money to start her own club in Kyoto, far from her hometown. "I came from Okayama. I graduated from high school and then went on to study *ikebana* [Japanese flower arranging], tea ceremony, and other traditional Japanese arts. Coming from a fairly refined background, I found it hard to swallow my pride, and that's something you have to do constantly in the *mizu shobai* business."

But that's not the only problem that can plague a club's mama; there are also predators who seek out the weak in the *mizu shobai*. "I hate gangsters. I won't let them into my club. There are a lot of sleazy guys out there. You get a girl into your place as a hostess, and then some guy comes in and lures her to another club. I've been tricked many times." Despite these problems, she has managed to keep a handful of loyal workers. "I have five girls here, one of whom has been with me for sixteen years, another for ten. The shortest time any current hostess has been here is three years."

Another drawback of the *mizu shobai* business is that a mama's presence is required almost every night. Unlike office workers who can take vacations and have their work covered by others, the mama of Opulence and others like her don't feel they can afford to leave their businesses unattended for long—and the stresses of working with very little time off take their toll. "I really want a vacation. I've had ulcers three times." And there are money concerns: The mama of Opulence has never married, and she's had to support her parents. "My father died last year of a long illness, and the hospital bills are expensive. On top of that I've had long stretches of barely breaking even as well as running in the red. To bring in new customers, I'd have to freshen up this place, but I can't afford to do it.

"In Kyoto, when asked how business is, most people answer with a vague, 'so-so.' They could be on the verge of bankruptcy, or they might be making a fortune. People aren't straightforward in Japan; even friends don't tell each other real problems most of the time. Stress builds up, and there's nowhere to turn."

The mama of Opulence sounds as if she's ready to wave the flag of surrender. "You have to call up customers constantly to get them to pay and to get them to come into the club. I also have to deal with angry wives who call about husbands having affairs with hostesses. I tell them that if one grasps too tightly to a kite it won't fly. Kites need to be given a little slack. Sometimes the wives may be calling about something that isn't even true. I've been doing this for a long time, and I'm tired."

TAMI-CHAN

In strong contrast to the understandably downbeat outlook of the mama of Opulence, Tami-chan glimmers with energy. Her perky, childlike personality earns her the affectionate suffix of "chan" rather than the more formal "san." She's not particularly attractive; as an avid tennis player and golfer, her thin, athletic figure would not earn her the label *guramaa gyaaru* ("glamor girl") among her peers. Her clothes tend to be on the far side of what many people would consider tasteful, and she's more likely to jump up and do an impersonation than she is to glide elegantly across a room. But despite these seeming drawbacks for the *mizu shobai*, she was a very successful hostess who went on to become the mama of her own place.

"Being beautiful is how a woman feels, not so much how she looks," Tami-chan says. "A girl can have a great face and wear the most expensive makeup and still not be attractive. On the other hand, a woman endowed with less who feels good about herself and does the best she can with what she has can be very appealing." Tami-chan is a prime example of her own theory. As a hostess, she consistently brought in customers from her own circle of regulars. She's entertaining, candid, and at the same time manages to make customers feel as if they are being mothered and supported. Cheerful and energetic, she can belt out a song with *karaoke* (literally, "empty orchestra," background music provided for customers to sing along to) better than most.

Now in her mid-thirties, Tami-chan is an accomplished professional. She has mastered many of the fine arts that make a *mizu shobai* woman successful, and she has smiled most of the way through. "I started out as a bunny girl when I was sixteen. [Bunny girls are cocktail waitresses dressed in skimpy outfits, reminiscent of Playboy Club bunnies.] You have to be eighteen by law, but I got in. I switched to being a go-go girl, then went back to being a bunny girl." After these early ventures into the *mizu shobai* world, Tami-chan became a hostess.

"I thought being a hostess would give me a chance to talk with a variety of people. In the club scene, everyone is on the same level, so I can talk on easy terms with a company president, which I couldn't do in a daytime job. I also enjoy the challenge involved in dealing with a lot of people and different situations; it keeps me on my toes."

Money is one of the motivating factors for anyone in the *mizu shobai*, but Tami-chan never speaks directly about that aspect. As do most other hostesses, she values the independence afforded by her work. "I feel sorry for housewives who have never done anything on their own, whose lives blow up in their faces at forty. What can they do? They're totally dependent on their marriage or family." Tami-chan was married for a few years when she was in her twenties. "I think the breakups that occur in hostesses' marriages have a lot to do with their husbands' understanding of the situation. This is a business that deals with the opposite sex. If a husband can accept that with a clear head, I think a hostess can make a wonderful wife."

Tami-chan believes that special aspects of Japanese society created the *mizu shobai* business. "Compared to women in other countries, Japanese women are very poor at entertaining at home. The typical couple gets married and has just enough room for themselves and two or three kids. There may be room for relatives to drop in or for close friends to come for mahjong, but not enough for formal entertaining— inviting two or three couples over for a dinner party, for instance. That's why we have nightclubs in Japan. A hostess is like a substitute wife. Without that feeling, customers wouldn't come."

Tami-chan's description rings true, even for the customers who come into a club to entertain business clients. They want to please clients by showing them a good time, and having attractive women serve them makes them feel at home, as if they're being taken care of and pampered. There is a parallel in the image of the 1950s or '60s American couple who would invite people home, with the wife expected to be the perfect hostess.

For the man who visits a club privately, the substitute wife scenario is even truer, because a hostess acts even more as a wife-girlfriend-mother figure with non-business clients. "A hostess has to judge a customer's mood on any given night just by glancing at him when he walks in the door. If it looks as if he's in a good mood, she might be fun and energetic; if he looks down about something, she may listen to him quietly. Knowing how to keep each individual happy is part of the job."

Where American businessmen tend to take their clients out for lunch, the emphasis in Japan is on evening entertainment, because that allows more opportunity to drink alcohol, and alcohol is a key factor in loosening up otherwise stifled ideas and feelings. "In Japan, when a big contract is in the works, somehow having women on the scene softens the atmosphere; it sets up a kind of rapport between the dealing parties. I think it's good to combine masculine and feminine qualities to make business work. In an extreme case, a businessman might say to his customer, 'I'll give you a woman if you'll sign the contract.' We would never send a girl out to meet a customer at a hotel for a deal like this, but there are clubs that do."

Men often pay more for a couple of hours in a moderately expensive club talking with hostesses than they would for a prostitute or on a visit to a "soapland," one of those bubblebath brothels that used to be known as *toruko*, short for Turkish bath. "If a man just wants sex he can go to those places. When a man comes to a club, he's buying the feeling that an encounter might happen. We supply the material for a man's dreams and desires. Being able to keep a man believing that he has a chance, a possibility of making love, and yet always tactfully turning him down in such a way that he enjoys his time, is a hostess's true talent."

Even for someone as upbeat as Tami-chan, *mizu shobai* prejudice is an issue. "When a wife comes into a club, you really feel that she's looking down on you. Even if you don't have anything going on with her husband, she looks at you with daggers in her eyes. *Mizu shobai* women are constantly surrounded by men, so they get a bad reputation." Prejudice has historically made it difficult for *mizu shobai* women to marry, but as Tami-chan points out, they don't always have a desire to. "Having so much experience with a variety of men, a woman develops a very good eye for who will make a desirable partner. Unfortunately, if she's in the business too long, she starts to see all men as fools. Even the most important, influential men of society act like babies or idiots at clubs, which leads many *mizu shobai* women to lose any desire to marry."

Tami-chan has two children, though she doesn't speak of them often, since they are in the custody of her ex-husband. Perhaps this separation from her own children has something to do with her future goals. "I never really wanted to become the mama of my own club, but circumstances allowed me to have a place of my own, and friends said that I ought to try it once before I left the business, so I'm giving it a shot. Ultimately, though, I'd like to be a nursery school teacher. If I had the money, I'd like to run my own school. I'd like to work with little kids as I get older."

Whether Tami-chan ever actually makes the move from club mama to nursery school teacher is for the future to tell. In the meantime, she continues the life she knows best, in the realm of bars and men. Although it's her livelihood, she has thoughts about how Japan might rid itself of the need for its thriving bar, entertainment, and sex industry. "I think husbands that fool around or go to these clubs are responding to their wives' lack of effort in their sex life. Soaplands and pink salons make sex fun. After a couple has two or three kids, sex is for enjoyment, not for reproduction, but the average wife may not live up to a man's needs, or she may refuse to engage in *shakuhachi* [a bamboo flute, slang for fellatio]. I think Western women want to enjoy sex too, so they put more effort into it.

"When a couple first gets married, they have a sexual relationship, but after they have kids, that disappears. As in ancient times in Japan, the woman evolves into housekeeper and mother. The man works long hours, eats late dinners, and hands the paycheck over to his wife. She takes the money and brings the kids up with it. That's it." Tami-chan has suggestions for improvement.

"We don't have babysitters in Japan the way other countries do; people don't feel it's right to leave their kids with someone outside the family. That's silly. Kids will grow up just fine if you feed them and teach them right from wrong. They don't need their mother hanging over them every second. Couples should leave their kids with relatives or a neighbor and get out together, or leave the kids somewhere else and just enjoy making love at home, chase each other around the house and scream if they want. If married couples would do this for themselves, maybe hostess bars and soaplands wouldn't be necessary. I'd like to get a bunch of housewives together and tell them that!"

Chapter Three

THE GEISHA WORLD

For three of my five-and-a-half years in Japan, I lived in a rented room for which there were no bathing facilities. Like many other residents of Japan's older towns and rural areas, I had to make a daily trek to the public bathhouse to bathe and wash my hair. Many of the women I encountered there got used to seeing me and occasional other white Western bathers, but there was always someone who was not used to seeing a foreigner. The common experience of being pointed at, stared at, and commented on was hard to escape in a bathhouse, where everyone undresses and bathes in large open rooms. I was usually treated kindly, but was also taunted to the point of tears on one occasion, and to the point of silent anger on many others.

One day, as I was pouring water over my head with the plastic water bucket used for scrubbing and rinsing before entering the large, steaming group baths, I noticed from the corner of my eye that other women were turning their heads to look at something, some of them murmuring in low voices. Used to being the object of stares and murmurs, I couldn't help wondering what was drawing everyone's attention. I turned to see a very young woman with her hair pulled up and back in a traditional geisha style, stepping demurely through puddles to an open set of faucets, partially hiding behind her bucket and washcloth.

Murmurs turned to silence as this young woman quietly sat down to start her bathing ritual. Her back was the focus of all eyes: On her neck, trailing toward her back, were the traces of two spikes of white makeup, most of which had already been removed. These revealed that she was a young apprentice geisha, taking a morning bath after an evening of entertaining in the teahouses of Gion or Pontocho, centers of Kyoto's traditional as well as contemporary night life. I felt that it was natural for me, a foreigner who would rarely have a chance to see something as rare as a real *maiko* (apprentice geisha), to have an uncontrollable urge to look at this woman, but the fact that these Kyoto women also were in a state of awe toward her surprised me. What I didn't realize then is that the geisha world is hidden not only from outsiders—like foreigners—but also from the vast majority of the Japanese public.

The realm of the traditionally trained geisha has enormous mystique in Japan, and represents the pinnacle of the *mizu shobai* world. The top-level, first-class modern hostess clubs may offer tasteful conversation, exquisite food, and fine music, but they cannot offer what the geisha world has to offer: hundreds of years of tradition. Guests who spend an evening in a geisha teahouse, preferably one of ancient Kyoto's traditional houses run for generations by the same geisha family, enjoy the finest in Japanese traditional dance, accompanied by the twang of the *shamisen* (traditional Japanese stringed instrument), and the singing of bittersweet *nagauta*, or long, epic songs. These are all performed by highly trained artists, the name geisha literally meaning "art person." (In Kyoto, geisha are referred to as *geiko*, a more colloquial, affectionate term.) Conversation may range from international politics to the fine points of a particular cuisine, and all is spoken, at least in the geisha districts of this Heian-period (794–1185) capital, in the soft, deferential Kyoto dialect.

All of these forms of entertainment are offered in the company of kimono-clad geisha and *maiko*. Young geisha wear pure white makeup and wigs in imitation of their sisters from centuries past. *Maiko* also wear white makeup, but they wear no wigs, instead having their own hair professionally fashioned into the distinctive *maiko* style. Geisha past their mid-twenties move on to a more subtle, mature look of less dramatic kimono, flesh-colored faces, and their own hair in a more modern pulled-back style. And what else do these women offer? In the back of everyone's mind is the nagging question of whether geisha "do it for money," but in short, no, true geisha do not have short-term sexual relationships for money. A visit to an *okiya*, the office-residence of young *maiko* and geisha during their training, gives a view of the preparation involved for an evening of teahouse parties.

Kneeling before an antique mirror, a girl of seventeen in a dishevelled blue and white cotton robe contemplates her freshly washed face and prods her carefully arranged, stiff, black hair with a long-tipped wooden comb. Easily mistaken for a wig, Satomi's hair is professionally set twice a week. Between settings she must sleep on a special pillow that raises her head and keeps her hair from being crushed. Next to her on one side sit Mickey Mouse and a giant stuffed *tanuki* (a Japanese raccoon dog); on the other side kneels twenty-year-old Fumiko, preparing to apply makeup to her face. Fumiko, having recently undergone *erigae* (the change of the under-kimono collar, symbolizing graduation from *maiko* to geisha), wears an elaborate, neck-straining wig, styled in the manner of her Edo-period (1600–1867) predecessors.

Making up for the night begins by rubbing on a layer of skin-protecting oil from the chest up. Foundation in a shade of bubble-gum pink covers the entire face, but is soon almost completely covered by a brushed-on and then briskly patted layer of stark white. The pink seems to have been unnecessary until one sees that a hazy, rosy glow has skillfully been allowed to emerge in strategic places on the face. Satomi and Fumiko take turns meticulously sponging onto each other the double-spike design that decorates the nape of the neck. The white from the back is adroitly buffed to blend with the white that's been painted on the shoulders and chest, and all is blended evenly on the neck and jawbone.

In a room of her own across the hall, Makiko sits in front of the mirror, various utensils and pots of cosmetics at her fingertips. Her eyes rarely leave the mirror, her business requiring her to scrutinize her own face each day to live up to the expectations of customers eager to be served by a true Kyoto *geiko*. Makiko is twenty-one, also having undergone the collar-changing rite. Satomi appears from next door to apply white to Makiko's back and neck, and the *okaasan*, the geisha's housemother, a tiny woman approaching seventy, helps Makiko into her kimono.

Makiko answers all questions about her life in one-word utterances while applying translucent red oil to the corners of her eyes. How old were you when you came to Kyoto to become a *maiko*? "Seventeen." Where did you come from? "Kyoto." Come on, where did you really come from? "Osaka." (*Maiko* and *geiko* of Kyoto are determined to give the impression that they were born and bred there, though the vast majority come from rural areas or distant cities.) Did your parents approve of your becoming a *maiko*? "No." Is the life what you expected it to be? "No." When do you see your friends and family? "Holidays." How many days off do you have a month? "Two." Will you continue as a *geiko* in the distant future? "Yes."

When makeup, wigs, and kimono are set, the *okaasan* dexterously ties the constricting, waist-binding *obi* for the three girls, showing amazing strength in the face of a strenuous task. The *okami-san* (proprietress) of the *ochaya* (teahouse) where the girls will entertain tonight comes up the narrow dark stairs to pick up the girls, who don over-kimono, delicately patterned with maple leaves and cherry blossoms. Feet clad in white *tabi* (special socks with big toe separate) slip into the traditional thonged sandals awaiting them at the door, and these four colorful shapes shuffle off under paper umbrellas in the last afternoon light; lavender, crimson, olive, and indigo melting into the glow of early evening.

GEISHA IN HISTORY

These geisha are part of the traditional entertainment world of Kyoto's Gion, an area that reaches from the Kamo river on the west, to Higashioji Street on the east, and arguably as far north as Sanjo street and as far south as Gojo Street—though in official geisha registries Gion is just one section of this wide area. What better place for geisha, keepers of a flame of tradition, than this traditional district of Kyoto. It contains a number of notable landmarks, including Kenninji, the city's first Zen temple, established in the beginning of the thirteenth century; Minamiza, Japan's first theater, established in the early seventeenth century; and the well-known Yasaka shrine. Yasaka, originally called Gion shrine, was regarded as a protector of the cotton merchants who once dominated the area. The Kamo river was long used to rinse the dyes from cloth made in the fabric and kimono trade. At one point in wartime, even the luxuriously living geisha were forced to help with silk and cotton production in exchange for being able to work in the evenings. The shrine is still the scene of crushing crowds at the New Year and is visited by people enjoying nearby Maruyama Park, where some of Japan's most breathtaking cherry trees bloom every April.

For all ranks of Japanese society, from the imperial family to the lowest paid field workers, cherry blossoms have always been a symbol of beauty. This was true in the days of the samurai and their ladies of pleasure, and it is true today. Gion's geisha and *maiko* have long brightened Kyoto's spring with a series of what were originally advertised as the Cherry Dances. In 1872, dances such as the *Miyako Odori*, *Kamogawa Odori*, and *Kyo Odori* were established. These dances are still performed today. Geisha and *maiko* were originally requested to dance publicly to contribute to the good of the community.

A brief look at the history of the Japanese sexual entertainment industry will give some perspective on today's geisha. During the almost three-century-long Edo period, the shogun, or top military general, reigned over the capital city, Edo (now called Tokyo). Contact with the outside world was almost completely forbidden, allowing or perhaps forcing Japan to intensify the development of its own cultural idiosyncrasies and specialties. The powerful shogunate government controlled every aspect of life: jobs, travel, food distribution, and even pleasure. Since many men stayed single their whole lives while fulfilling their duties to their lords, prostitution was seen as a necessary service. Men who couldn't afford prostitutes had to be satisfied with looking at *shunga* (literally "spring pictures," a combination of characters using the same sexual euphemism as *baishun*, or "selling spring," meaning prostitution), the erotic prints that are censored in Japan today (even while the porn magazine and movie businesses boom).

There were four officially recognized "pleasure quarters" during the Edo period: Yoshiwara in Tokyo, perhaps Japan's best known historic pleasure district; Shimabara in Kyoto; Shinmachi in Osaka; and Maruyama in Nagasaki. The Japanese word translated as pleasure quarter is *yuukaku*, a word composed of the two characters for "play" and "wall." This is a good representation of what these quarters actually were, walled enclosures where women were kept for sexual play, the entrances and exits guarded so that this profitable property could not escape. Many young girls were sold to pleasure quarters by impoverished parents from the countryside who had to feed the rest of their starving families. Unofficial, smaller pleasure quarters existed along travellers' pathways and in some small towns, but they were neither recognized nor approved by the government.

Geisha thrived during this period. Originally dancing girls providing musical and visual entertainment at parties, geisha progressed to the stage of pouring sakè for guests, and then to sleeping with them. In the early days of the Yoshiwara quarter, there were men and women geisha, literally artistic entertainers. The women were strictly prohib-ited from having sex with the customers; in fact, their services were not even needed, because there was already a healthy supply of yuujo, literally "play women," for men. Taiyu and oiran (high-class licensed courte-sans) also provided sexual services. The original taiyu courtesans, particularly famous in Kyoto's Shimabara district, had their own form of dance and music with which they entertained customers, but as their artistic skills decreased, the demand for geisha became stronger.

In 1712, teahouses were granted licenses so that geisha could enter-tain in the area now known as Gion, and Shimabara prostitutes complained that the "non-prostitute" geisha were taking away their business. Still, at this point women geisha were also engaging in sex with customers, and some who called themselves geisha did not have any particular talents other than a capacity to entertain beneath the bedcovers. These *gei nashi no geisha*, "geisha without an art," remained popular until the end of the Edo period. If they didn't have an art, what did they have? Their skills are artfully captured in a haiku-based *senryuu* poem from the Edo period, *Shamisen no heta wa, korobu ga joozu nari*, whose literal translation is "Those who are bad at the *shamisen*, become good at falling down." The geisha who couldn't play the *shamisen* or dance well became good at lying down with customers.

The decline of the Edo period started with the destruction of the shogunate. Samurai were out of work, they had no lords to serve or support them, and even men of rank had no way to make a living. The gap between rich and poor became greater, prostitution thrived, and the four original prostitution districts were far outnumbered by cheap, renegade brothels at inns and by small local prostitution houses. The entertainment business in the Gion area survived a number of bans and reopenings by the government until the late 1800s, when the more open policies of the Meiji period (1868–1911) brought in Western influence. As time went on, the true, artistic geisha separated them- selves completely from the *gei nashi no geisha*, who gradually evolved into café girls, dance-hall girls, and bar hostesses.

A morning stroll past the traditional wooden houses south of Shijo street, the best-preserved section of Gion and home of the most traditional teahouses and geisha living quarters, takes one back in time to the Kyoto of countless decades ago. Simple plant arrangements sit in front of windowless walls and closed lattice doors. Small "Post No Bills" signs defy the publicity-thirsty poster hangers whose colorful banners plaster almost every bare space in the city. Often the only sign that one of these silent houses has people inside is an empty milk bottle outside the door. Simply written characters in the doorways represent the name of each establishment, and are the only hint that these are centers of evening entertainment. This is the quiet simplicity and refined elegance, the *wabi-sabi* aesthetic, that pervades traditional Japanese culture.

Moving north to Shijo Street and crossing at Nawate Street, one is dazzled by the glass and neon that glare in the morning sun as brightly and harshly as they do at night. The multi-storied buildings that mark this part of Gion provide a sharp contrast with the quiet area south of Shijo. Boutiques and expensive shoe shops are still closed, but the paper lantern shop is open, marking the entrance to a tiny street leading to Onoya, a teahouse where Satomi, Fumiko, and Makiko often entertain. This tiny street and its teahouse are anomalies in this ultra-modern, neon-club neighborhood, which nightly fills with hostesses running to work and customers searching for an evening's pleasure.

A Geisha's Story

Onoya's *okami-san* is tall and graceful, and doesn't look her forty-four years. "I'm a third-generation geisha. I was born three years before the war ended. My mother had been a geisha for a year when my father became her patron, her *mizuage danna-san*." *Mizuage* refers to a geisha's first sexual experience. *Danna-san* literally means master, but most commonly refers to a husband. In the geisha world, it refers to the man who becomes a geisha's formal patron, who sponsors her activities with money and also takes her on as a mistress. "I was born a year later. He said he wanted her to marry him. To become a real wife in normal society my mother had to quit the life of a geisha.

"My grandmother was running a geisha teahouse then. She agreed to let my mother marry and leave if they promised that their first-born daughter would become a geisha and carry on her teahouse. And so I was brought up from the start in the teahouse in Gion, and my brother and sister were raised in another part of town. People really are different based on the way they're brought up. My sister works at a bank. My brother followed in my father's footsteps at a precision instrument company."

Onoya's *okami-san* explains that contemporary geisha don't suffer from the discrimination and shame that entertainment trade workers of past decades did. "My sister married into a very wealthy, respected family. When my parents met the family, they very clearly told them about my working in Gion as a geisha, and they said that if I wasn't allowed to go to the wedding, they wouldn't allow my sister to marry into that family. As far as I'm concerned, everyone has his own work or business, and one is no better than another. I don't think working in the *mizu shobai* is a problem these days. Being a hostess is just another occupation. People are in the business because they like it. The old dark image of girls going to Gion and becoming geisha to support their families is gone.

"My grandmother was born in the Meiji period. She was a geisha until she met my grandfather. She quit being a geisha to run her own *ochaya*. But just because someone is a geisha doesn't mean she will run her own teahouse. A patron has to buy her a house to run it in. My first *danna*, my *mizuage danna*, whom I met at nineteen, bought me this house. We had two children. We were together for sixteen years, and then we separated. In our hearts, we geisha are married to our *danna-san* just as the rest of society's wives are married to their husbands, but it's not the same legally. It's a recognized position within our realm.

"My last *danna-san* died three years ago. I'm not really lonely. I have my work, and my two children. I enjoy myself. Everyone is very supportive. People know about geishas' patrons, so when my *danna-san* died, everyone gave me their condolences. Of course, no one tells the wives about geisha mistresses. We can't be open about it. Recently, gossip magazines like *Focus* ran articles on famous men's private lives. I think that's wrong. Some mistresses talk to the press about wanting to marry their patrons legally. In the old days, people kept their mouths shut."

This proprietress knows the pain of having to be the hidden woman, even in the face of her lover's death. He was a well-known, high-ranking politician who lived in Tokyo. "I couldn't go to his wake. When he died, I found out about it on the news. I went to Tokyo right away. His secretary reserved a room for me at the Imperial Hotel, where I always stayed. I wanted to go to the funeral. I couldn't believe he'd really died; I had to see reality for myself. I'd talked with him just hours before. His secretary and friends thought about it and said that I could come if I didn't wear a kimono, which would set me off as being different, especially in Tokyo. I said 'Yes, I understand,' but I went in a kimono anyway!" The proprietress of the Onoya laughs as she remembers.

"I had to wait an hour and a half just to make an offering of incense. That was hard to take after having been with him for so long. I couldn't stand out in the crowd, couldn't cry. My *danna-san*'s secretary and friends used to come to the teahouse in Tokyo with him, so they knew me and recognized my position with him, but at a funeral, certain proprieties and ceremony must be observed, so they couldn't acknowledge my presence. It doesn't matter how many years two people have been together, in that situation, the mistress can't come out in the open. It would be wrong to cause problems for anyone. That was the one time

I saw his wife. I already knew his son; he used to accompany his father on trips abroad. He would never say anything about the affair directly, but acknowledged it in a silent way."

Isn't isolation from a loved one at death a high price to pay? "Sure it's lonely being in this position, but I understood that from the start. There's nothing to be done about it."

Despite the fact that the *okami-san* controlled her emotions and was discreet in paying her respects, the affair was discovered. "He had a photo of me in his wallet, and it must have been found in the hospital. He died suddenly, so someone must have gone through his things there. Also, as my *danna-san*, he would send me a monthly allowance. It's the same as a husband bringing home the salary to his wife. He didn't like the idea of giving me the money directly by hand, so he opened a bank account in his own name and put money in it for me. He didn't have any work or connections in Kyoto that would justify having an account there, yet every month the same amount of money was sent to Kyoto. That's how it was found out. The secretary called and said the account would be closed, but the suspicious evidence was already out.

"I didn't have trouble when that money was cut off because I run my *ochaya*. There are other geisha who quit working and live in an apartment rented by their lovers, so when something like this happens, it's tough. I always tell others that they have to keep working in some form or another. Women can always come back to being geisha, though. Wives legally have support if their husband dies. Being a mistress is not a secure living."

Being a mistress was even tougher in the old days. Most of the time, a young geisha in the pleasure quarters was assigned a patron, even if she didn't like him. She didn't get to choose. "Nowadays, a *danna-san* is the same as a lover, but of course he must have resources, or it's no good. It's no longer the case that a man supports a woman because she's a geisha, but that he likes her and she happens to be a geisha."

The rules of the geisha world have changed in a number of ways. "In the old days, the *erigae* collar-turning ceremony when a *maiko* became a geisha, was done only when there was an official *danna-san*. Now there doesn't have to be a *danna-san* to have *erigae*. For a *mizuage* ceremony, everyone gathers at a restaurant to celebrate. It's kind of like a wedding reception. The geisha and *danna-san* are officially introduced as belonging to each other in a union that's recognized within the geisha world as a marriage."

Some people see geisha and hostesses as serving the same function. They're both *mizu shobai* women entertaining men. "Really traditional people in the geisha world don't want to be compared that way, but looking at geisha as superior is just one viewpoint." The distinction doesn't lie just between geisha and hostesses, but also between geisha themselves. Kyoto has six *hanamachi* [literally "flower towns," meaning geisha districts]. All of the geisha and *maiko* within these districts are listed with the official registry, which keeps track of geisha affairs. "Each group has its own distinct customs and activities. Having dances and tourism is a big thing for some districts. I don't see any reason for antagonism between *hanamachi*, but some people feel that their own area is the best, that they have the only true *maiko* and geisha.

"As far as I'm concerned, we all are representatives of Japanese tradition. Judgments shouldn't be made by which district a *maiko* or geisha comes from, but on how talented she is. If someone can dance well, she needn't be embarrassed anywhere. Instead of talking about others, geisha should study and practice their own art." One of the most derogatory terms in the *mizu shobai* vocabulary is *onsen* geisha, or hot-spring geisha, referring to the women who serve men at large resort spas. They refer to themselves as geisha, but are considered to have little artistic talent except for satisfying a man's most primal desires.

The *okami-san* of Onoya ran a club as well her teahouse for many years. "When I split up with my first *danna-san*, this was still a club with around fifteen hostesses. I have another house across the way that used to be the teahouse. My kids and I lived on a floor separate from the club, but the kids could always hear the customers and hostesses and see them coming in and out. Three years ago, on the fifteenth anniversary of the club, I decided to change it. My last *danna-san* rebuilt it for me. Now the other house is where I live, and this is the teahouse.

"Economically speaking, it's hard to say which is better, a club or an *ochaya*. To run an *ochaya*, however, you do have to own an entire building, so that makes it harder. There are some geisha who run their own snacks. In the short term, it's easier to run a club or a snack, and there are many more of those than there are *ochay*a." But the long-term prospects are better for a teahouse proprietress. "A club mama can't do very well at fifty or sixty, whereas the *okami-san* of a teahouse can be seventy or eighty and it doesn't matter.

"The basic act of entertaining—whether at a teahouse or a club—is the same. When there are a lot of customers at a gathering, geisha sometimes work with *kompanion* [young women hired to be warm bodies at parties, not expected to have the artistic skills of a geisha or even the conversational skills of a professional hostess]. Some geisha treat the *kompanion* like dirt, but when my geisha and I entertain with them, we get along fine. That's the best way to keep the party happy. We're geisha, but they're there for the same reason. The same people that are snobby about which geisha district they came from turn their noses up when they have to be in the same room with *kompanion*. For a geisha, having a *gei*, or an art, is the most important thing. There are some *maiko* who act uppity these days, but the three girls at my place aren't like that. I don't teach them that way of thinking. Attitudes get passed down from the *okami-san* to geisha and *maiko*."

Being from Kyoto is also considered a matter of pride among geisha, but hometown *maiko* and geisha are not so easy to come by these days. "I don't think there are any teahouses left where all of the *maiko* are right from Kyoto. Girls come from all over. Even if a geisha has a daughter, there's no guarantee that she'll become a *maiko*. My daughter is a third grader now. In seven years or so, she can become a *maiko*. If a geisha has only male children—which many of them do—she may end up having to sell the teahouse. It's still not that unusual to have families like mine where there are three generations of geisha, but there are a lot of people who quit."

Though the thought of having one's daughter continue the teahouse is appealing, it's not so easy to accomplish. "It takes a lot of money to set a daughter up to be a *maiko*. The kimono alone are expensive— ¥20,000,000 wouldn't be enough to buy everything." Contrary to what many may think, geisha do not make an inordinate amount of money purely from their party engagements. Much of the money they make is given directly to the manager of their *okiya* for room, board, management of their affairs, and clothing expenditures. Any big money there might be comes from either running one's own teahouse or from a patron.

"The girls get only some pocket money, and their house takes the rest. Without a great deal of money, a house couldn't outfit them in fine kimono. Everyone gets excited about seeing what kind of kimono a new geisha will wear to special events. Most of the kimono are specially made at a few select stores, and they are very expensive."

Geisha teahouses, like top-class clubs, follow the practice of accepting as customers only men who have been introduced by another trusted customer. "I can refuse to accept anyone. For the most part, though, if a new person isn't the type to match the atmosphere here, he won't be introduced in the first place. Customers think about it before they introduce new customers, because they have a real responsibility. Geisha customers don't change teahouses very much. There's a strong link over time. When a customer comes in, he'll also introduce his son as a customer. We have third-generation customers, and we've even had guys bring in ten-year-old sons for a visit, asking us to take care of them when they're older."

Though the traditional Japanese food usually served at teahouses is primarily accompanied by sakè, whiskey is also served. The same system that exists at clubs—each customer keeping his own bottle of whiskey at the bar—is also in practice at modern teahouses. "At my teahouse, there are well over four hundred bottle-keeps. If it's a big company, there might be a separate bottle for each department, or even for each executive. It sounds like a lot of bottles, but we have men visit from Okinawa, Tokyo, Hokkaido. Some visit Kyoto only once a year. We'll keep a bottle for them for years."

Not only do men come from afar to visit the geisha of Kyoto, but the geisha of Kyoto also go long distances to offer their services. "Next month I'm going to Okinawa for three days. We have to take all the kimono and things for the *maiko* and me. Recently I went to Tokyo, Niigata, and Hiroshima. In May we'll go from Sendai to Nagasaki. I don't tell our regular customers that I'm gone. The others really work hard when I'm away to keep the customers happy. There's no difference in the *ohanadai* [literally 'flower money,' meaning the hourly geisha fee] between working at home or away on a trip, but if I'm making money on a trip and other geisha are entertaining at my teahouse, I'm making money in both places."

As much as trips to exotic locations sound like fun for *maiko*, the path of a geisha is not an easy one, and should not be lightly chosen. "Girls come to Kyoto on school trips, see *maiko*, and become infatuated with the image. They want to come and learn to be a *maiko*, but they won't make it if that's their only reason. They have to really like dancing or whatever art they choose. Some girls spend two months learning how to look like a *maiko* and then get sick of it and quit. After going through the training of a *maiko*, they have to train to become geisha. They don't have any free time. Office ladies have evenings and Sundays off, but a geisha has commitments all day long, and often on weekends. What would be free time is taken up with dance or singing rehearsals and the like. *Maiko* have to get their hair done during the day. It's tough just to pop into a movie with that hairstyle. It is a restricted lifestyle in many ways.

"It seems as if geisha are dressed up all the time, but most are really pretty casual if they don't go out. I'm in the habit of getting up at 8:00 in the morning because my children have to go to school. Then I spend the rest of the morning arranging flowers, doing the accounting, and cleaning up. Usually I have two days off a month, unless there's a special gathering or event. Most people have the first few days of the year off, but look at this calendar—most of the New Year's vacation is filled with engagements. Many Sundays are filled, too. I have only one day off in February, and we're already booked up through May. And these are reservations; we also have people call in every day who want to come in that night.

"I try to spend as much time as possible at home during school holidays to be with my children. Parties don't start until 6:00, so there is time together until then. If I go to a movie, it's usually a cartoon with the kids. It's great fun being with them, but it's tiring! There always seems to be something that needs to be taken care of for the parties. Getting dressed takes time. Sometimes I have to make special preparations for a special kind of food for a particular customer or group. I have to plan for those things. I really don't have a lot of free time."

Onoya's *okami-san* is busy with her business and children, but what about time for herself? Doesn't she want someone to share her life? "I'm too old to get a new *danna-san* now!" she laughs. "It's nice for a woman to have a man in her life, but not just anyone can become a *danna-san*; a good lover doesn't necessarily qualify. A geisha and her *danna-san* have to confer on things, visit sick people, call on people together at New Year's. It's a big responsibility. But being recognized as the *danna-san* of a geisha of a particular house or district makes people think a man is really something. In a sense, having such an affair found out is almost a matter of prestige. A *danna-san* is treated differently from other men."

Even though the word geisha implies a devotion to an art, in the end the geisha world is a business. "You can't do this as a hobby; it's a business. You have to be very good at switching back and forth between personal life and work. Customers don't come in to hear about your problems, they come in for their own dreams. No matter what happens to me at home, even in the short distance it takes to walk here, I have to switch out of that mode. I can't let my feelings out, can't show anger to customers. There are geisha who show those feelings, and they get bad comments from the customers."

What about the customers that are so annoying to hostesses, the men who get grabby and make rude comments? "We don't get really obnoxious customers at the teahouse. For customers who really don't know how to behave, I have the *maiko* sit next to me and demonstrate to him how he should behave. There are some difficult customers who talk about nothing but their work. For young *maiko*, it's difficult to adjust. Their legs ache and they get sleepy and even say so sometimes. Here, you have to quit talking about work. You have to be able to talk about a variety of things. You have to be able to see what kind of person a customer is quickly. We can't be perfect, though. With dozens of customers coming in every day, it's impossible to remember everyone's name. Sometimes there are parties of fifty."

As the *okami-san* said, being a geisha is a business. Beyond the mystique and air of tradition, there are yen signs waiting to be added up, though discussing money in the geisha world is done tastefully. "We can't figure out each geisha's *ohanadai* until the evening's over. We send bills—we don't get paid in cash—so we have to have responsible customers. Customers ask how much *ohanadai* is per hour, but it's hard to pin down an exact price. It all depends on how many customers and *maiko* there were, what kind of food there was, and so on. When a customer asks how much an evening is going to be, I tell him it's hard to judge until the evening is over, and then I ask him how much he wants to spend. That way I can adjust the evening to his resources. On a really busy night, a geisha might be booked up, and if some customer wants her at his party no matter what, he has to pay extra. It can be more expensive during busy times and cheaper when things are slow. Having a geisha dance is included in *ohanadai*.

"If the whole time for the geisha to leave and get back home is over two hours, the *ohanadai* might be around ¥24,000. That all depends on the place and the geisha. It's not really firm. I don't change my prices according to customer. If a *maiko* or geisha likes a customer in a party in another room that she hasn't been called to, she might just pop in to say hello. Lately, the *maiko* are choosing the customers instead of the other way around! Hostesses can make good money, but they have to be young, so the number of years they can work is limited. Age doesn't matter for a geisha, as long as she has an art. There are seventy-year-old geisha still working. They get the same *ohanadai* as a *maiko*."

The *okami-san* is optimistic about the geisha business. "Teahouses aren't going out of business because of the poor economy as some of the clubs and bars are; a teahouse will close because an *okami-san* gets old and there's no one to follow her footsteps." Are there enough geisha to satisfy the potential *danna-san* of Japan? "Out of about three hundred geisha and *maiko* in Kyoto, there are only about seventy *maiko*. That's not enough. There's a stage at which many quit. One becomes a *maiko* at seventeen or eighteen, then a geisha at twenty. Many quit at twenty-four or twenty-five. A geisha might decide to quit on her own, or her *danna-san* has her quit. Maybe he doesn't like having to wait while she's out at parties, so he buys her an apartment to live in. It's an age when people think they can do other things."

No matter what a woman decides to do with her life in the long run, Onoya's *okami-san* believes that the path of the geisha is a wise one to choose, even for a short time. "Women who have been *maiko* are at an advantage, not just those who go on to become geisha, but those who go on to university or to work at a company. They have a sense about the relationship between men and women.

"I feel good about my life so far. I do wonder about what direction my children will go in. I guess there could be some prejudice against geisha children, since they are illegitimate, but in this era, I really don't think it's that important. As for my son . . . well, in a teahouse, the son doesn't have a real connection with the business. Some geisha sons work at the nearby shrine, others work at the *danna-san*'s business, though I can't do that with my son. If my daughter goes off to be married, I'll still be here. I'd like my daughter to become a *maiko* and geisha. I think it's the best life for a woman. Of course it's up to her to decide, but I will encourage her to follow in my footsteps."

Chapter Four

A SPECIAL KIND OF SLEAZE

After my first walk through the narrow streets of Gion to find the club through which I was to enter the hostessing world, I got used to seeing the countless flashing signs and hawkers who tried to entice clientele into their lower-class dens of sexual satisfaction. "Only ¥2,000 for twenty minutes! Girls, girls, girls! Come on in, big boy, there's a nice young girl waiting for you! No drink minimum!" I walked quickly through these areas to the high-class clubs, afraid that I would be mistaken for someone on her way to one of these cheap sex places. The hawkers sometimes called out to me, but I ignored them and walked on. I tried to convince myself that what I was doing was far above this low-level business; I was working in the upper echelons of the club world.

One night at a party in my boarding house, I told two young Japanese men—one an ex-coworker from a language school and the other my future husband—that I was working at a club, and they immediately kidded me about working in the nightclub business. I didn't take the chiding very seriously at first. "What kind of clothes do you wear, a bikini or a bunny-girl outfit?" I was shocked that they thought I could possibly work in one of those lower-class places, and told them so. I explained that I worked at an exclusive top-level club, and that the women all wore relatively conservative, expensive clothing, nothing risqué.

Since they didn't frequent Japanese nightclubs of any rank, this distinction didn't seem to mean all that much to them. Fortunately for me, they considered my working there a lark, a kind of short-term adventure for someone on foreign turf. It seemed clear, however, that though those of us working in elite clubs considered ourselves in a completely different category from the women working in the cheap sex bars, there were many people who saw no distinction at all.

THE EJACULATION INDUSTRY

There are certain risks to working in any *mizu shobai* business in Japan, but the women who keep the limbs of Japan's sleazy sex joints flexing probably take the biggest risks. The low-ranking entertainment establishments that I hurried by make up a multi-million-dollar industry within the *mizu shobai* known as the *shasei sangyoo*, or "ejaculation industry." Top-class hostess bars sell atmosphere and the feeling that a sexual or romantic encounter may happen, while ejaculation industry establishments sell real sexual encounters, visual and physical, for much less money than it costs to have a drink at the best clubs. It is puzzling to many Westerners why Japanese men pay more money for a couple of hours of drinks and conversation than for explicit sexual services.

Satisfying men's fantasies is the forte of the constantly evolving ejaculation industry. There are the pink salons, no-panty coffee shops, Turkish baths, peeping rooms, health massage parlors, date clubs (including *sekuhara*, or "sexual harassment" date clubs, where men can come in and harass women dressed like office workers), mistress banks, S & M clubs, and live-sex-on-stage strip theaters. These are only some of the many places men can go to be sexually entertained and serviced. When describing hostess bars and geisha teahouses, people usually qualify their description by saying that the women who work there are not prostitutes—prostitution defined here as having one-night stands with customers for cash. Even if a hostess chooses to go to a hotel with a customer, top-class club management does not get officially involved with such activities.

The women of Japan's ejaculation industry establishments, on the other hand, are not only encouraged but in most cases required to have short-term (ranging from twenty minutes to a number of hours) sexual relationships with their customers. As the industry's name implies, men don't come to these places just for the atmosphere. The women who work in the ejaculation industry often seem to have less of a specific purpose or goal in having chosen their work than the women who work at high-class places. This may not be true of all women when they started, but the common pattern is to enter the seamier side of Japan's nightlife with the intention of making big money and getting out quickly, and then ending up not being able to leave at all.

Keiko, 20, works in Kabukicho, Tokyo's most notorious entertainment district, known for *yakuza*-run bars and sleazy sex joints. "I first started working here when I was still a student. I worked at a no-panty coffee shop [where, as the name implies, waitresses wear no panties under their skirts]. Most of the time I just served coffee, but they had a back room where we took guys who wanted special service. They paid extra, but we'd make sure they were satisfied, and in fifteen minutes we were back out in the front room. Even when I was really young, none of that really bothered me. I kind of liked it." Signs on the walls made it clear that customers could expect to have an orgasm, but no intercourse. "I never had a guy at that place try to go beyond the limit. I guess I was lucky, because sometimes other girls had to call in waiters to stop the guys."

Keiko learned early on that the sex business is lucrative. "I made a lot of money at that no-panty coffee shop. I bought expensive clothes and accessories, and a car. I was too young to buy a car myself, so I gave a friend the money to buy it for me." Money buys not only merchandise, but service. "I went to host clubs [where women pay to be served by men] after work and enjoyed myself. I could have the nicest-looking guys and the best whiskey at my table, even though it was expensive. I love going out and splurging on myself and my friends."

When law enforcement slowed down much of the wilder *mizu shobai* activity in the mid-1980s, Keiko took a job selling clothes at a boutique during the days. "I had a really high energy level. I was so hyper that I decided to work nights, too, and then I'd stay up partying all night after that. I smoked and drank like crazy and didn't eat or sleep much. I was a wreck. I could barely see or talk straight." Keiko got so weak and sick that she could no longer get up to go to work. After spending two months in the hospital for exhaustion, Keiko went right back to her old life of working nights and partying until dawn. "I quit the day job, but I still get tired. I don't go back to the doctor even if I feel bad, because I know he'll just tell me to stop smoking and to rest more. I can't. This is the way I am."

Keiko has fallen into the same patterns that many other ejaculation industry women do. "Everything I do is with cash. I make cash and I spend cash. If I make money, even a lot of money, I go out and spend it having a good time drinking with friends. That's what I like. I know that other people build up savings accounts, but that just doesn't mean anything to me."

EARLY DAYS

Keiko is one of the many modern women who offer men sexual satisfaction without being categorized as hard-core prostitutes. The "world's oldest profession" has existed in Japan as far back as history is recorded, but the contemporary ejaculation industry really got started around the time World War II ended. A turning point in Japanese sexual mores occurred at that time, changing Japan into a world of sexual freedom, not only for men but also for women. The *ianfu* ("comfort girls" assigned as prostitutes to comfort and entertain soldiers) of Japan switched from comforting Japanese soldiers to earning desperately needed money from the American Occupation Forces. Though these women who hung out on streets and in bars wearing heavy makeup and provocative clothes and calling out to Americans were derogatively called "pan pan girls" by their fellow Japanese, they were in many senses true survivors. For many, having this work had become a matter of life and death, for themselves and their families. From this unfortunate beginning, the women who had the strength to break away from their feudal ties and sell themselves to foreigners started a kind of general sexual freedom, and in some ways, social freedom for women.

A key step in this sexual freedom started in 1947, when a new kind of entertainment for Japanese men, the strip tease, began to develop. Strip shows in Japan originated in a theater in Tokyo's Shinjuku district. Women posed on stage as if in a picture frame, forming a tableau of some famous painting. They in fact still had underwear on, and the curtain would stay open for a mere fifteen seconds. During these early days of sexual entertainment on stage, that fifteen seconds kept the packed audiences in awed, staring silence. Though the underwear gave way to a thin wrap on the bottom and nothing on top, the novelty of this early strip show wasn't to last long. The spiraling thirst for the next sexual gimmick and thrill transformed these shows, and the transformation goes on to this day, creating some of the wackiest ideas in sexual entertainment imaginable.

These still, picture-frame shows progressed to shows with dancing and stripping, but the women still didn't actually take off all their clothes. The phrase "strip show" was used for the first time in Japan in 1948, and the use of the Western phrase was another sign of modern thinking entering a once-closed world. Strippers were called *libe-chan*, or "liberal girls." These scantily clad liberal girls not only danced but also poured drinks. The shows were so popular that crowds overflowed and men from the audience were forced up onto the stage. Even Kyoto's ancient and revered Minamiza Theater had strip shows in 1950. Popularity shifted around this time to what were known as "nude shows." Originating at the once thriving and famous Nichigeki Music Hall, nude shows were similar to the big dance numbers in Las Vegas, in which nearly nude women dance and parade on stage.

As customers grew familiar with the standard strip shows and nude shows, new gimmicks were needed to keep men coming in, such as a famous "snake lady" stripper, acrobatic strippers, and Caucasian strippers. Having white women as part of the strip show became necessary for Japanese strip shows to survive, and it wasn't until around 1980 that the trend shifted away from needing a white woman on stage to keep customers happy. In Tokyo, strip shows were fairly low key, while Osaka and Kyoto went to new extremes. In 1956, Osaka had the first strip show where pubic hair was actually shown.

This is significant in a country where to this day there are troops of censors who flip through imported magazines and movies, carefully scratching out any signs of pubic hair, a touchstone for determining what is truly pornographic. A children's comic book can graphically depict a violent gang rape, but this is not considered pornography as long as pubic hair doesn't show. On the other hand, no matter how artfully or tastefully presented, an image in which pubic hair appears is officially censored.

Tokyo followed Osaka's lead with these more explicit shows later on. The sexual directness and gimmicks grew and expanded with time. Today, the variety of shows advertised to entice viewers is mind-boggling. Imagination can guide one to picture the special features of lesbian shows, tease shows, bed shows, *Tengu* masturbation shows (Tengu is a folklore goblin, represented by a mask with a very long, phallic nose), cutting board shows (where a woman is displayed like food on a cutting board being prepared for eating), animal shows, and S & M shows.

At some point in the gimmick progression, adding comedians between stripper performances became popular, much as in American burlesque. Many of Japan's current popular comedians got their start working in between strip acts. After the first two main phases of Japan's strip show history—the semi-nude, picture-frame phase followed by stage shows making anything imaginable visually available to the audience—the final step to live sex shows was made. In a live sex show, a stripper does her regular act as a buildup to the grand finale, in which a member of the audience volunteers to come up on stage and have sex with her. Even this became passé, however, so now it is not unusual to have many customers on stage engaged in various sexual activities.

Live sex shows took on a life of their own separate from strip shows. The most extreme category may be the live S & M shows with members of the audience participating. Posters advertising "live enemas on stage" are not difficult to find among all the other colorful ejaculation industry advertisements. There are plenty of S & M clubs that don't have stage shows, but do offer a wide range of S & M adventures. This is another part of the *mizu shobai* in which women can say they are not actually prostitutes, for most of the women who work at these clubs do not actually have sex with customers. A woman must become proficient at using a whip, giving enemas, dripping hot wax on body parts, anal manipulation, bondage techniques, and talking in a manner that makes the customer feel "bad"—that is to say, good. This may not be a complete list of services, but it covers the basics.

As one S & M club "queen" says, "It took me a while to get used to doing the things we do here. At first it seemed kind of strange. But now I've decided that everyone has at least a little bit of sadistic or masochistic character to them, it's just that some people are extreme. Most of the men that come here are not ashamed about it, at least not within these club walls. Our clientele ranges from truck drivers to company presidents." Surprising as the existence of these clubs may be to outsiders, many Japanese citizens themselves would also find it surprising to know just how many such private S & M clubs exist throughout their country.

SOAPLAND

A look at Japan's famed *toruko* gives a view of the more hard-core side of the ejaculation industry. *Toruko*, or Turkish bath, is the old name for Japan's prostitution bathhouses. In the mid-1980s, there was enough pressure from the Turkish government to make Japan stop using this term, which the Turks considered degrading to their national image. *Sopurando* ("Soapland") is the term devised by the Japanese to erase the word *toruko* from their vocabulary, but the existence of the bathhouses themselves was not erased.

What was it that so incensed the Turkish government? Soaplands are establishments with a series of private bath rooms in which a customer is treated to a lavish array of bathing, massage, and sexual services. If prostitution has been illegal in Japan since 1958, how can there be such a huge number of prostitution bathhouses? These places are registered with the authorities under the classification of "private room bathhouse." It's not that the authorities don't know what really goes on in these places, but Japan has a long history of letting this kind of business go along until there is some reason for a special crackdown. Immigration authorities make the rounds to ferret out illegal immigrants working in such places, but most soaplands run without police interference by keeping their non-bathing activities low profile.

The non-bathing activities at a soapland depend on the establishment. Most men are given a choice of how elaborate they want the service, and this is reflected in the price. As one soapland manager describes it, "A full course at our bathhouse lasts 90 minutes. It costs ¥12,000 for the bath fee and ¥30,000 for the special service. The girl gets to keep ¥27,000." What does she do during that 90 minutes to earn her ¥27,000? The customer enters the private bath room, and his hostess takes his clothes off and hangs them up. "The first part of the service is *shakuhachi* [fellatio]. Then the girl gives the customer a bath." Japanese baths involve scrubbing one's body outside the tub before soaking in the clean hot water, and most people sit on a low stool while scrubbing. Soaplands are equipped with special chairs that support the customer while at the same time leaving space for the woman to place her head below his body. "At this point she licks the customer's anus and fondles his testicles." This must be a real challenge when soapy water is falling into her face. "After the chair, she gives him the human sponge treatment." The customer lies on a mat to be massaged by the woman's lotioned and soaped body. "After she rinses him off again, they move to a bed for the real thing [regular sexual intercourse]."

The manager discusses the business side of soapland. "Our girls usually take in five or six customers a day, and work twenty days a month." This calculates out to a healthy monthly average of nearly ¥3,000,000. "The girls here are responsible for buying their own work equipment, including lotions, soaps and shampoos, and condoms." Women are assigned their own individual bath room and can decorate as they please, many surrounding themselves with stuffed animals, proof that Japan's "cuteness mania" doesn't stop even for the most adult activities.

One soapland worker, Maki, 33, has spent years living on the edge. She has a track record of theft and prostitution, and has been beaten, stabbed, raped, and robbed over the years. Years of dating bikers, *yakuza*, and *yakuza* tattoo artists (she herself has a large carp tattoo on her back) helped get her started on this track. "I've dated regular guys, too. Businessmen, guys with daytime jobs." Maki has never tried working during the day, and takes pride in the professional skills she has developed in her night work.

"I worked in the best resorts, like Ogoto [a giant sex resort on Lake Biwa, in the Kansai region of Japan], and am known for my superior techniques." Maki expresses scorn for the people around her, using her sexual skills as a badge of honor to promote herself. "These young guys don't know what to do with their own dicks, so they come to soapland to have someone show them. Men know they can get whatever they want here as long as they pay for it. Most of them are afraid to ask their girlfriends or wives to do anything other than standard sex. I've slept with company presidents and gang bosses, and everything in between. No matter who it is, though, I'm always the one in charge. I'm the one who is teaching them something. The other girls here don't have much experience. Some of them take a lot of crap from customers, too. Guys yell at them and abuse them and they think they just have to sit there and smile, never standing up for themselves. After they've been in the business long enough, they learn how to defend themselves, both physically and emotionally."

Even someone as experienced as Maki has seen some strange things that bother her. "I have one guy who has been following me around for years. He's an idiot, a real country bumpkin. He's like a lot of the guys who come to these places, unattractive, can't function normally in society. No matter how many times I change jobs, he finds me. I've heard other women say they've had similar experiences, but this guy seems pretty extreme. I've thought about telling the police about him, but then again, I could get in trouble, too. There are a lot of strange guys who come to soaplands. I keep a knife in my bag just in case someone gives me real trouble."

Not all soapland workers are as tough as Maki. Aki-chan, a bright-looking 28-year-old who has been a soapland worker for four years, doesn't carry the hard edge of many other sex-industry workers. "My mother was widowed and had to take out a big loan a few years ago, and she couldn't pay it back. I figured that if I worked at this kind of job I could make enough money in less than a year to pay the debt off. Instead, things just got worse." Her mother thinks that Aki-chan is working at a classy hostess club in Ginza, and often calls her at work. "The people at the front desk here answer the phones as if it's a club, but I'm always scared that she's going to find out the truth. I don't know what she'd do. I have friends working here who are married, and their husbands know about their jobs. Some of them don't care, I guess."

Aki-chan knows that to make money she has to service men. "I tell my customers that I'll let them do it without a condom if they request me by name, because I get more money that way." Many women use this technique to maintain their popularity, but with the concern over sexually transmitted diseases, particularly AIDS, this is not a wise way to win a popularity contest. Aki-chan's natural kindheartedness seems a waste in her working environment. "I try to help the new girls who come in. Some of them don't know what to do, how to use their bodies for scrubbing or how to use the special chair and shower equipment. I teach them to help make things easier on them, and before I know it they're gone. It's lonely here, even though I see so many people every day at work. We get a lot of disabled men. They're often nicer than the other customers. Sometimes I spend extra time just talking with them. I think they're lonely, too."

Suffering from chronic respiratory problems, Aki-chan is often tired at work. "Some days I get worn out just thinking about the first customer coming in. I break down and cry for no reason." Aki-chan is like many other women who dipped their feet into ejaculation industry waters intending to get in and out quickly for a specific financial goal, but then for one reason or another, found themselves trapped. Murders of women in this business are on the increase, an unfortunate occupational hazard, and perhaps a sign of changing times in Japanese society.

The women of soapland represent the hard-core, professional prostitution side of the ejaculation industry, but many other businesses offer women who exude more naiveté, and in doing so, have lured a whole new range of customers to the ejaculation industry.

AMATEURS

A major step in the trend toward attracting men to clubs with "amateurs" instead of "pros" came in 1978 when the first *noo pan kissa*, or no-panty coffee shop, opened in Kyoto. Like the simple thrill of the original still-picture nude shows in the late 1940s, the mere fact that women were not wearing panties was an attraction in and of itself.

Osaka's first no-panty coffee shop opened in 1979, and things mushroomed from there. What was the great attraction? Until this time, the other sex-oriented entertainment places were literally and figuratively dark, with no windows. The fear of the unknown and the gloomy image intimidated many men. The same image problem prevented young women from working at these places. No-panty coffee shops, however, were well lit and had windows open so that you could see inside. A cup of coffee was ¥700—expensive for coffee, but nothing like the price of going to any of the other sexually oriented bars. Young college coeds who wanted to make good part-time money but didn't want to do anything hard core could make two or three times the hourly wage that any other waitress could make simply for not wearing panties while they served coffee.

In the opening months, there were long lines of men waiting to go into these shops, but again, the men's attention waned. They were not satisfied with simply looking up a mini-skirt every time a waitress bent over to pick up an ashtray or clean a table. Soon, topless no-panty coffee shops came into fashion, and mini-skirts were replaced by scanty fabric draped on the hips. At the peak popularity of no-panty coffee shops, one establishment in Osaka went all out by installing a water tank in which a girl swam around in nothing but her panties (which apparently disqualified her from serving coffee). Another place built a room under the shop in which customers could come to watch waitresses walking above through two-way mirrored floors. Theme shops opened, each with its own specialty. One place had waitresses with thin towels wrapped around their hips serving coffee from buckets similar to those used at public baths.

The popularity of no-panty coffee shops peaked in about two years. By 1980 there were topless and bottomless shops with every gimmick imaginable, but the public had lost interest. There are still some shops left, but not anywhere near the numbers there were in the no-panty heyday. The cycle of sex business popularity moved on with a new trend which started in Nagoya, the *noo pan massa*, or no-panty massage parlor. As Keiko described earlier, not only could a man look at the waitresses, but he could also go into a private "massage room" for fellatio or manual stimulation. The soft-core ejaculation industry's point of brilliance is satisfying men physically at a low price while keeping women attracted to the work by not having them engage in sexual intercourse.

The second boom of popularity for no-panty coffee shops came with these private massage rooms. Peeping rooms where men look through a two-way mirror at a woman who strips, poses, and masturbates also became popular. All of these places had their range of variations and gimmicks. Strong competition brought on some very creative, though short-lived ideas. There was one unique place advertised as a "coffin coffee shop" with "porn fortune telling." A customer entered and found dry-ice smoke surrounding a white coffin. He took off his clothes and entered the coffin, which had two strategically placed trap doors, one at the face, and the other at the groin area. After awhile, a naked woman appeared and opened the trap doors to play with the "corpse." She used the lower trap door to play while the man watched her from the upper-body trap door. Telling each other's fortunes was another play option.

Many of these places make Japan sound like a sexual amusement park, and in some ways it is. The idea of offering quick, cheap satisfaction without a woman ever having to show her face was another innovation. A number of places sprang up in which a man could step into a booth that closely resembled a department store dressing room with a curtain to be closed behind him. On the walls of the booths are "glory holes" encircled by crudely drawn nude female bodies with poster cut-outs of the head of some Japanese singing starlet. The main feature is a conveniently placed hole in the wall at crotch level. A customer walks in, drops his pants, puts his penis through the hole, and holds onto the hand grips on the wall while looking at the face of the starlet on the wall. Some places also provide sexual sound effects on headphones. On the other side of the wall is a woman (no guarantees here) who deftly brings him to a climax by hand. A sign at the upper corner of the booth says, "After wiping you clean with tissues, we clean you once more with a wet cloth, so feel free to put yourself back into your pants as is."

"Fashion health" massage parlors offer inexpensive satisfaction without actual intercourse but with much more contact than the "glory holes" offer. Some places will let a customer pick his partner by looking at a group of women through a two-way mirror or by a TV monitor or photos, but other places offer no choice. A fashion health worker explains the rules. "The girls are nude, and the men can touch them. There's no intercourse, but oral sex is allowed. A girl decides herself whether she lets a man finish in her mouth, or whether she even does *shakuhachi* unless he wears a condom. Guys pay anywhere from ¥5,000 to ¥15,000 for twenty to fifty minutes at our place."

Mayumi, 22, works at a fashion health parlor. There is little pretense of making conversation. Customers go with a specific goal. "Guys don't care about making small talk at this place. They want girls, and they want them young. We get a lot of *Lolikon* types in here." *Lolikon* is short for "Lolita complex," commonly used in Japan to describe older men in search of sexual partners of a tender age. "The work is easy. When I don't have a customer I take a nap. I like my work; no one is forcing me to do it."

Mayumi is involved not only in the sex industry, but also with drugs and gangsters. "My friends and I do a lot of speed. That's pretty easy to get a hold of. We can get other drugs, too. My boyfriend and his friends are part of a biker gang, and he gets us lots of stuff." In Japan, even simply being accused of a drug offense can mean becoming an outcast from society. "I've never been in any trouble with the police myself, but my boyfriend spent a year in jail." Mayumi has a more hard-edged personality than most customers want at a place where they go for the feeling of an innocent amateur. Even she can put on a good show, though. "I giggle a lot, and act shy. They love it, and I just laugh about it later."

A wave of morality law crackdowns closed down many of these establishments in 1985. Hawkers were no longer allowed to step outside of their doorways, signs could project only so far into the sidewalks and streets, and time restrictions were imposed on drinking and entertaining. These morality laws seem to be aimed at stopping the spread of "immoral" businesses, but more than that, they protected the existing shops by curbing the overwhelmingly fast-growing competition. By 1990, the downturn in these businesses caused by the strict laws had turned around on itself, and business started picking up again. The strong yen has attracted women from all over the world to earn money in such centers of iniquity as Tokyo's Kabukicho. More than ever before, women from Taiwan, Thailand, Singapore, the Philippines, Denmark, Brazil, China, and other countries can be seen heading to work in bar districts. It is the foreign element that is the source of Kabukicho's current sense of excitement.

Some of the many gimmicks and types of business that spring up in the ejaculation industry actually catch on and remain in some form or other for a number of years. For instance, telephone clubs found tremendous popularity starting in the 1980s. It sounds ridiculously simple, but it seemed to find a niche in the hearts of many Japanese looking for company. Similar to the 900-number phone businesses in the United States, Japanese telephone clubs make up a pay phone system that allows men and women to talk on the phone and arrange dates if they wish. The typical "club" is run from a small set of rooms in which men come in and sit with a phone. As one phone club worker describes it, "Men pay an initial fee to join our club. After that they pay ¥3,000 for the first fifteen minutes and then ¥500 for every fifteen minutes after that. Girls can call in for free. If no girls called in to the toll-free number we advertise, we wouldn't have any business." Women simply call the advertised number, and a guy waiting in one of the rooms picks up the phone. "If two people hit it off, they can arrange to meet somewhere. After that it's up to them." By 1990, the phone companies in Japan listed over a thousand such phone services.

Worth mentioning here are what are commonly called *kyaba kura*, or cabaret clubs. These are similar to regular hostess clubs in many ways, except the women are young and amateurish rather than the polished professionals of a regular club. The women don't have to perform oral sex, as they do in other ejaculation industry places, but many cabarets do require the hostesses to perform on stage. Some places billing themselves as cabarets go so far as to have live sex shows, but most places that go by the name of cabaret are not so hard core. The young women aren't allowed to be too good at dancing and singing, because it's the amateur atmosphere that appeals to most cabaret customers. Some cabaret clubs also have special themes or certain days of the week when the women have to wear a certain type of clothes, like a "tennis look" day, or a leotard day. Cabaret customers are mostly salarymen, but could also range from sumo wrestlers or monks to gangsters. From a cabaret hostess's perspective, "A desirable customer is one who isn't rude, gives good tips, stays for a short time, and doesn't ask to go to a hotel." There are very few customers who meet all of these requirements. Most women in the *mizu shobai* realize quickly that they can't be picky if they want to make money.

PINK SALONS

Cabaret workers have it easy compared with their sisters in the pink salons. Pink salons, in Japanese *pinkku saron*, are registered with the authorities as the same type of business as a cabaret—a drinking-related business—but the women are expected to give more of themselves. Pink salons have been referred to as "conveyor belt processing facilities for sexual desires." This description fits many ejaculation-industry businesses, but it fits the pink salon business especially well.

By law, pink salons are not allowed to perform any sexual services for customers, but in reality they do. These places, which look very much like cabarets, with booths for customers to sit with women, also have a distinct difference: the smell. Rather than the usual mix of alcohol and tobacco smoke, the aroma of the pink salon has been described as a mixture of perfume, semen, and disinfectant.

This peculiar mixture is of course produced because most customers go into pink salons with the intention of having a sexual interlude. The lighting is dark, the music is loud, and inside the booths, it is hard to see or be seen by other customers. A man can request a particular girl if he's been to a place before, or he can be assigned a girl when he enters. Girls are given tables according to when they punched their time cards. First in, first to get a customer. Once a girl arrives at her customer's table in her provocative costume, a waiter brings whiskey or beer and light snack food. He also brings a substantial number of wet towels for preliminary and post-action clean up. Drinks and conversation are not the main focus of the visit.

Men pay by increments of time, perhaps starting with forty minutes and paying more for each twenty minutes beyond that. A talented pink salon hostess will get the conversation rolling so that the customer is just comfortable enough to unzip his pants and start enjoying the service at the time the next time increment is about to start. A man in the throes of ecstasy is not about to pull up his pants and leave before reaching a climax. A less sophisticated pink salon hostess will unzip a man and start right in as soon as he sits down. This is not considered quality service. Pink salons suffer from stiff competition, and in some places, what was once supposed to stop at fellatio went further. Some of the young girls who enjoyed the job as long as they didn't have to have intercourse quit if that was expected of them. If they wanted to go that far, they could make a lot more money working at a soapland.

Many of the young women who work at pink salons come from Japan's rural districts. Yuri is a typical case. "I came from Shikoku Island. A girlfriend and I thought it would be exciting to come to Tokyo. It's a big city and we figured we could get exciting jobs." Morality laws prevent direct advertising of sexually related businesses, so pink salon want ads usually list a need for companions, floor ladies, lounge ladies, bunny girls, dancers, singers, or even office workers. "When we saw an ad in the paper for a job that paid well and included a dormitory, we called right away. We didn't have anyone to stay with in Tokyo, and we didn't have money for a hotel. The ad said they needed hostesses, so we figured we'd be pouring drinks and talking with the customers. When we got there for our first night, we were shocked."

Yuri and her friend had a chance to observe the club and its activities before they were assigned booths, and they realized they were not in a regular hostess club. "I'd had a couple of boyfriends back home, so I knew what was going on, but the thought of putting just any guy's thing into my mouth was disgusting." No one knows at what point the magic wand waves over these young women and makes them decide to stay, but Yuri and her friend decided to see if they could get through one work day. "I didn't like the thought of touching guys like that, but figured if I was going to do it I may as well plunge right in. My girlfriend and I went at it full force from that first night."

Yuri lasted at the first place for only a few days. "I worked at a regular bar for a while, and after that I fell into letting a guy take photos of me for a porn magazine. Somehow that seemed easier. I got tired of that quickly, though. By that point, my friend had already gone back to Shikoku. I tried working at a bar again, but the money wasn't all that good. Now I'm back working at a pink salon. I don't have to worry about what to say to the guys. They come in and sit down, and the whole thing is over quickly. I don't know how much longer I'll stay here, but I can't really go back home, either. I'm still trying to think up a story to tell my family about what I've been doing all this time in Tokyo."

Mari, an attractive 22-year-old, also stepped into the pink salon world by accident. Like Yuri, she answered an ad for a part-time job in the evenings. "The guy that interviewed me convinced me that I should give the job a try. I guess I got confused. I knew what I was in for after I saw what the other girls were doing, but at the same time, I thought I could just close my eyes and get through it. I didn't have any other job prospects and the money sounded good. On my first night I went into the bathroom after every customer and rinsed my mouth out. I hated it at first, but when they handed me my first night's pay in cash I decided to do it full time. It's great money."

Mari has saved money, and lives at home with her parents. Like many soaplands, her pink salon has a phone which is answered as if it is a regular bar. "My fiancé doesn't know that I work here, either. I'm trying to save up money for our marriage ceremony. My parents can't pay for a really nice wedding, but I want to have the best. I can make almost ¥600,000 a month here if I get enough regular customers. It won't last forever, and the money is a lot better than my old office job."

Keeping enough women in pink salons isn't easy. Many places spend from ¥1,000,000 to ¥3,000,000 a month advertising for workers. As we have seen, by writing only "bar hostess" in their ads, they mislead women who don't mind serving drinks but who do mind looking at a new erection every forty-five minutes. Men workers are also necessary to keep pink salons running, but it is a job that many men find distasteful. To slow down the turnover of waiters and doormen, some pink salons promise waiters a promotion to manager at three months, then from manager to director in another three months. This all works out because the waiters, managers, and directors all do pretty much the same job, and by the time the men at the director level realize that, they are ready to quit, which makes room for the lower-level workers to move up. The larger chains of pink salons have a company system almost as elaborate as many large corporations.

Some pink salons have a nightly pep talk bordering on cult religion rhetoric for all the workers, with loud military marches blaring to keep up employee spirit and lots of ritualized manager and employee statements and responses. A military-style roll call completes the nightly preparations for opening the salon. To keep employees feeling like part of a larger organization and to keep them motivated to work, some chains even have regular district meetings and competitions between branches. Gung-ho bosses with tears in their eyes scream out to their hostesses that they are relying on the girls' good service to push their shop's sales above the competitions'. Even some of the hostesses respond with tears to the emotional pleas of their bosses.

Group spirit has to be maintained to some degree simply for pink salons to survive. The waiters and other men who work at these places have the side task of going out to paste up posters and flyers to advertise their salons. Since advertising for pink salons and other sex places is illegal, they go in groups of two or three so that one guy can look out for the police while the others paste up the posters. Teamwork comes into play again when suspicious-looking groups of men come to a pink salon door trying to act as if they come to these places all the time. This is usually a sign of a police raid, and the doorman, who signals the number of customers coming down the stairs by the number of buzzes he pushes from his button at the door, gives a special buzzer signal to alert the staff downstairs that there will be a surprise police inspection.

By the time the undercover cops are down the stairs, the lights have been turned up and trouser flies have been zipped.

Police have cracked down on and closed many pink salons, as they have many of the other establishments in the ejaculation industry. History does repeat itself, however, and as mentioned earlier, 1990 was a booming year after a five-year lull in the business as a result of the 1985 crackdown. Though many of these places cannot be called houses of prostitution, they appeal to the same basic needs and desires, and as long as sex doesn't go out of style, Japan's ejaculation businesses will continue to thrive, underground or not.

Chapter Five

CUSTOMERS

 After I quit working as a hostess, I was a frequent customer at hostess clubs through business connections as a teacher, editor, and writer. I had always wondered how customers could stand to be treated in such an obsequious way by women who were obviously boosting their egos as part of their jobs. As a customer, I found it interesting to see the difference between really talented and run-of-the-mill hostesses.

As the guest of important male customers at expensive clubs, I was treated like royalty. Top-of-the-line hostesses could even flatter me, a woman who was obviously not paying for the evening's entertainment, in such a way that the compliments didn't seem insincere. No one lit my cigarettes, since I don't smoke, and no one hand-fed me, but my drinks were poured, and I was showered with flattering attention by hostesses and mamas. It was amazing how smooth some of these women were. Less talented hostesses, on the other hand, came off sounding cheap and empty.

Though there are different reasons for going to a club, for many it is an escape through alcohol and a search for temporary warmth and companionship. As a teacher of businessmen from Japanese corporations, I was often invited to go out drinking at the end of a set of classes. The company I worked for saw this as part of the working relationship, similar to taking each other out drinking to improve business relations. Seeing the transformation of a Japanese salaryman from a businessman-English student to bar customer was sometimes astounding. Shy, silent men who never spoke a word in class turned into aggressive pranksters. Men who seemed almost neurotic in their tim-idity became instant Don Juans once alcohol passed their lips.

I once went to a bar without hostesses with one of the quietest groups of students I'd ever had, from one of Japan's largest corporations. Not only did they boldly play laser disc after laser disc of soft porn in front of me, but one of the quietest students actually started making lewd remarks to me, and another asked me to dance. There were no other women in the bar, and when I refrained from dancing, thinking it was not the appropriate thing for a teacher to do, the young man stood up and started dancing with one of his male coworkers. This was their time for fun, and they were going to dance cheek to cheek, women or no women.

After any such drinking session, the next time I saw the students in class, there was never any reference to activities or jokes from the night on the town. They were back to their quiet, timid selves. The license and freedom allowed to Japanese when they consume alcohol is so ingrained within the social fabric that drinking is the main source of relaxation for many. "Let's go drinking" is by far the most common call to share a good time with friends, acquaintances, or business associates. But is this all there is to Japanese bar customers? Are they breast-grabbing, slobbering drunks, or corporate powerhouses making billion-dollar deals? Some of the customers of Japanese bars, clubs, and geisha teahouses are both. There are the company presidents who sip their whiskey at the most elite clubs and top-ranking politicians who enjoy a *tête-à-tête* with elegant geisha. There are John Doe salarymen who go out for booze and some laughs, and men from all walks of society who enter the soft porn realm of the sexually oriented cabarets and salons. Men who frequent *mizu shobai* clubs reveal why they spend their money at these places and what they see as society's motives for continuing the hostess and geisha worlds.

NAKANO-SAN

Nakano-san owns a number of small restaurants serving *okonomiyaki* (a cabbage and meat pancake, as popular among the Japanese as pizza is among Americans). Heavy-set, with wavy hair, large eyes, a moustache, and dark skin, Nakano-san could just as easily be taken for a Mexican as for a Japanese. As a restaurateur, he is considered part of the *mizu shobai* world, since his business also runs into the wee hours of the night, *okonomiyaki* being a popular snack food that many people stop for during late-night bar hopping.

"I go to clubs mostly for personal enjoyment, usually with friends," Nakano-san explains. "Many of my friends are my customers, so in that sense there's a business connection. Since I own my own business, when I spend money at a club—even if I go for business—I'm spending my own money. I don't run on a big company system." Nakano-san doesn't blow his money at the really expensive places. "At a snack or club, I spend anywhere from ¥10,000 to ¥20,000. I also go to cheaper places where they tell you exactly how much everything costs on a menu, which is unusual. At that kind of place a customer can figure out exactly what he's going to owe before he leaves. You never know at a regular club."

Nakano-san says there are ways to avoid financial embarrassment when going out for a night on the town. "If you're worried about the money situation, many big clubs will adjust an evening to the budget you set out if you call ahead. The big show clubs used to do that, but they're gone now. If you went into Bon Amour, you probably would have had to spend somewhere over ¥20,000. You were charged for the bottle keep, the food, and the number of girls who sat with you. It was much cheaper if you took a date and watched the show, without requesting any hostesses. If you really went all out, you could spend ¥50,000. Plenty of famous people went to that club." Nakano-san doesn't mention a notorious gangland shooting that took place there shortly before it closed. "Their price range was clearly laid out; they didn't change prices depending on the customer. If you had the best whiskey, ordered a lot of food, and called two or three hostesses over, you could spend a lot of money. In any club it's always more expensive if you go only with guys, because you're sure to pay for the company of hostesses. Then there's a *shimeiryoo* fee if you call a specific girl. That system isn't as common as it used to be, though."

What are the social patterns that go with drinking? It is unusual for a man to go into most clubs alone. "I usually go drinking in a group of two or three, but not more than four. If it's a little place like a snack where I could sit at the counter, I might go in alone, but not at other places. I go to a snack or club maybe once a month on average. I have about four places that I go to on a regular basis. I don't have a bottle keep at all of them; I often go in and just order a beer or two. Other times I might go out to a café bar instead, where you don't have to have a bottle keep. I don't have a bottle keep in Nagaoka, the town I live in, because I know so many people who run bars there."

Feeling the obligation to reciprocate patronage can be a strain. "If I had a bottle keep at one guy's place, I'd have to have one at everybody's place, or someone would feel slighted. That's why people who run bars and restaurants tend not to go to bars and restaurants near their own shops. If they go to one, they have to go to all of them. On the other hand, in Kyoto itself, especially in Gion or Kiyamachi, all the people from the bars tend to go to the place next door. They secretly promise to bring customers to one shop if they'll return the favor by bringing customers to theirs. They pass their customers around."

Though it sounds as if this system has the potential to increase the number of customers coming into a place, Nakano-san doesn't like it. "I have to keep a balance, to maintain some equality. I goofed once in Nagaoka. On my day off, I happened to stop at a bar run by one of my customers. The next time the mama of that bar came to eat at my place, she said, 'Thanks for coming to my shop the other day.' Another mama from a different bar happened to be there that night and overheard. She was insulted that even though she came into my place, I never went to hers. You go to a bar to relax, but if I go to a customer's place, I have to be on guard. It's more relaxing to go to a place run by someone who's not my customer."

Does Nakano go for the girls? For the whiskey? "I go to clubs for the atmosphere. Going to sing *karaoke* is one part of that atmosphere. I'm not all that crazy about drinking. It's not that I don't like it, but I'm not like the guys you see in commercials who sit alone reading a book sipping fine whiskey. I drink for social reasons. Guys who are really into drinking don't have to go out to bars for booze, they could sit at home alone and drink. People go to clubs for atmosphere and for hostesses. Talking with friends is also part of it. I usually enjoy myself, but there are also times when I feel I've blown money for nothing, that an evening at a club wasn't enjoyable at all."

What makes an evening worth the money? Nakano-san feels it is largely related to the talents of the hostesses. "Hostesses who are real professionals, who are good at making conversation and can talk about anything, are a real asset, but they are slowly disappearing. There are some at the first-class clubs, but at most snacks and bars, the girls just sit there and give one-word answers. If the customer doesn't lead the conversation, she doesn't say anything. Some people don't care as long as the girls are young. That's one of Japan's bad points. Geisha are different; they have an art, training, and a true professional spirit. They can't be mediocre. Even if customers sit there silently, a true hostess has to be able to create an entertaining atmosphere on her own.

"If a girl just sits there and says 'Yes' and 'Uh-huh' and nothing else, it's no different from sitting and drinking at home. There's a big difference between fun clubs and boring ones. The ratio of boring to fun places is getting bigger lately. That's why more people are going to cheap drinking places with friends. You can eat and drink and talk inexpensively. It's a trend. The only places that will survive are the places that really treat their customers well."

Social customs play a big part in the motivation to go to hostess bars. "In America, there has always been a custom of going out with friends of both sexes, being open and talking together. Until recently in Japan, it was socially unacceptable to go out with someone of the opposite sex; men had to go to bars to talk with girls. Now, the young people in

Japan don't feel a need to go to clubs with hostesses. They've become similar to Americans in that they feel free to go out in groups or with their own girlfriends. Besides, young people don't have the money to go to snacks and clubs, so the number of customers at those places is shrinking.

"In the old days, salarymen would go in a group to places where there were hostesses, but now they bring girls from the office with them. This trend started from the time I was a student, in the 1970s. Places that really take care of their customers, that offer 'skinship' [a popular Japanese slang word for being physically close] and good service, will survive. The mediocre places will go under."

What about the nagging some men get from their wives for spending time and money at clubs? And just what is the attitude of wives toward the women who work at bars? "I'm not married, so I don't have to lie or sneak around or feel bad about going to a club," Nakano-san says. "A long time ago people looked down on women in the *mizu shobai*, but that's not so true anymore. A lot of women now make a clear separation between their work and the rest of their lives, so it's not such a big problem. In my view, women who go into the *mizu shobai* with a clear goal of something they really want to save money for are terrific; I respect them. Women who just go in to make money and end up spending it without purpose, or who are only in the business for some kicks, are the ones who regret it. I don't have a sister, but if I did, I wouldn't mind her hostessing if she had a clear aim in what she was doing. I wouldn't like it if she was just floating along with no goal."

Upbringing has an effect on people's attitude toward the *mizu shobai*. "I don't think there's really a prejudice against marrying some-one in the *mizu shobai* anymore, either. That era is gone. I'll decide who I marry by the kind of person she is, not on whether she's a hostess or not. My parents are fairly liberated. They don't discriminate because someone is a hostess, a foreigner, or a *burakumin* [Japan's untouchable class, long the victims of harsh prejudice]. We believe people are people."

Age is an important factor in a hostess's career, and customers make their preferences quite clear. "Customers always make a big deal over the younger girls. It's only when they're young that they're flattered by the men. As a hostess gets older, the only way for her to do well is to run her own bar. It sounds bad, but it's not so strange for a customer paying money to say what he wants or prefers."

Nakano-san looks at the business from the woman's viewpoint. "If I were a woman, I think I could enjoy being a hostess. The best part is the money you can make. You also get to meet a variety of people. There are unpleasant customers, but in the service industry, you get better at handling people. Hostesses are selling flattery. The product being sold isn't the food or the drinks, it's the girls and the flirtatious mood they create. It's a matter of making the customer feel good and providing good service."

Nakano-san acknowledges that sex is a major factor in attracting men to bars. "I'm sure there are many people who go to bars with sex as the goal, though they go to high-class places for prestige and appearance. It seems strange for Americans to see Japanese spend so much money for an evening in a bar talking with hostesses without ever having sex. But when you have a girl right in front of you, you feel as if you can seduce her. Men go into bars with that expectation. It's different from places like Turkish baths, where a guy can go in and know he can have sex for money."

As Tami-chan described earlier, the hostess who doesn't ever sleep with a man but creates in him the expectation that she will keeps the man coming back, but this often just frustrates some men. Nakano-san thinks this is why things are getting tough for hostess bars now. "I go with friends, and they complain that we each pay ¥10,000 or ¥20,000 and don't even talk with the girls very much, let alone sleep with them. There are places where you can get sex for only ¥10,000. The more the direct sex business expands, the more difficult it becomes for hostess bars. There used to be a really dark image associated with going to a prostitute, but it keeps getting easier. In America, things are very clear, you can pay for sex as sex, it's clear cut. As Japan continues to be influenced by America, the same trends will happen here—there will be a desire for clearly defined businesses. Unless a club has really talented, beautiful women to talk to, there isn't much reason to go anymore. There are plenty of places now using gimmicks to attract customers away from the usual type of hostess bar."

The value of women over men in the *mizu shobai* is still clear. "Of course the hostesses make more money than the doormen and waiters. Customers go for the women, they're the product. The men have little value in the business. They make things and carry things, and that's it. That's why their pay is lower. I was a waiter when I was a student; the pay was only ¥200 or ¥300 per hour. It's up around ¥600 now, maybe more for late night, maybe ¥700 or ¥800 at a good place. The girls all make ¥1,200 or ¥1,300 an hour, and even more at the best places in Gion."

Club standards differ from place to place. The contrast between expectations in Nakano's town of Nagaoka and nearby Kyoto is strong. "Sometimes the mama of a club in Kyoto will try to get a girl from Nagaoka to come work for her, but none of the girls want to go, even though the Kyoto clubs pay well. In Kyoto, they have to buy expensive clothes for work; they might show up at a club and be told to turn around and go home because their outfit isn't good enough. That doesn't work out well money-wise even with a high hourly rate. Some girls figure that even if the hourly pay is lower, they're better off in a place like Nagaoka, where they can wear their everyday clothes, even jeans. Things are tight in Gion lately, and many places won't pay a hostess's taxi fare home anymore. Girls figure they might as well be at a small place near home than go all the way into Gion for the same benefits. That's one of the reasons there aren't enough girls right in Kyoto."

Nakano-san is also familiar with the less elite end of the *mizu shobai* world. "Near my Kyoto restaurant there's a date *kissa* [coffee shop], kind of like a soapland. They keep a low profile because it's illegal, of course. You go for a date and the girl will sleep with you. I know what kind of place it is, but other people in the neighborhood don't. One of the girls that works there comes to my restaurant. She's a regular girl; you'd never guess she's a prostitute. Until recently, you could tell *mizu shobai* women just by looking at their clothes; they had a special way of dressing. Now you can't necessarily tell at all. Some girls, college coeds and the like, are just doing it as a part-time job.

"I've introduced customers at the date *kissa*. Guys go in and look through photos of girls, and then the office sends a girl out to meet the customer at an agreed-on place. It's pretty expensive. They charge ¥30,000 or ¥40,000 for two hours. There are various systems for these kinds of places. There are a lot of *hote toru* [hotel Turkish baths] in Osaka's Juso district. They have rooms in apartment buildings where they send girls to meet customers. At a real Turkish bath, they use various techniques to wash the customer's body before they have sex. It's an art. At the hotel Turkish baths, it's just plain sex. They don't have any special techniques. The girls are amateurs, all they need is a desire for sex. They might be college coeds, regular girls, not pros."

Mistress introduction services are also popular in the sex business. "*Aijin* [mistress] banks have long-term contracts that specify charges for a year's relationship. Men pay a monthly allowance for a girl, maybe ¥100,000 or ¥200,000, and based on that, they can go once or twice a week to see her. They have to pay for dinners and anything else they do together. After a couple of meetings, they decide whether or not to go ahead and set up a contract, and they negotiate. They don't start out with set prices; that's decided between the girl and the customer. The girl has a right to say no, whereas at a date coffee shop, a girl can't say much about the customer even if she doesn't like him. She can't choose her customers at Turkish baths, either." Customers don't always have a choice, though. "At some Turkish baths there are photos so a customer can choose the girl, but not at all of them. If there aren't any photos it's tough for a guy to say he wants a different girl after she's already come into the room." Nakano-san doesn't mention that in the tougher neighborhoods, the customer who requests a different girl might get a visit from a burly bouncer who would discourage him from changing his mind. Money does talk, though. "You can pay more and have two or three girls at the same time, but that's expensive."

Although he runs a restaurant, Nakano-san finds the bar business appealing. "Running a restaurant is a solid business. I'll open another shop soon, but someday, I'd also like to try running a pub type of place—not a snack or club where girls sit with customers. I'd run a place with just guys working and doing the serving, with a nice atmosphere for men and women. Women are becoming customers, too. It takes research to find out what is currently making customers happy. Most snacks and clubs don't take the time to study those trends. Just opening a bar and having girls sit there won't work anymore. You have to look at the young people who are student age. What they'll like as they get older is going to be very different."

Nakano-san has seen the growing trend toward clubs that cater to women in the form of host clubs, "where men work to serve women. Most of the women who go are *mizu shobai* workers like Turkish bath girls, or women with older husbands who don't pay enough attention to them. There are a lot of those. The wife is still young, she doesn't get much sex at home, and she has money. She goes to a host club to have some fun with a young guy, someone who will spend time serving her, bend down to her orders. A host has to have something to make the women happy—he has to be able to do something like dance or sing, or he has to be good-looking. Since so many of the women who go to host clubs are from the *mizu shobai*, host club hours start late, from say 10:00 p.m. until morning. It's not all young guys, either, that work at host clubs; there are older men, too, to take the older women out. They have to show off for that business, so they wear big rings and fancy clothes; you can tell a guy's a host right off. Hostesses go there to get the same kind of service they give to men. Some women just go in to drink and enjoy the atmosphere. Sometimes they'll go out with a guy afterwards."

Nakano-san evades discussion of the widely known aspect of host clubs, which is that most of the men provide more in-depth service than can be performed in a bar. As one young man who worked as a host to pay off his debts put it, "I had to lick women in places I didn't even know they had." And to prove that men, too, have feelings, this same young man sometimes cried after work, a reaction to the degradation he sometimes endured during his working hours. This is not something most men, including Nakano-san, like to think about.

Still, Nakano-san is interested in the whole range of *mizu shobai* businesses, and looks at it all with an open mind. "The other night a group of customers came in around 4:00 a.m., and I realized that one was a famous transvestite from Kiyamachi. There aren't that many transvestite clubs around, really. You see guys dressed as women waiting for customers in the back streets; they call out when you walk by. There's kind of a shady atmosphere there. Places like host clubs and transvestite show clubs where *mizu shobai* workers go for entertainment suffer when the *mizu shobai* suffers. It's all part of the business."

HINODE-SAN

Hinode-san is well into his fifties. He is thin, with gray hair and bloodshot eyes. He wears a three-piece suit and works at a successful small company, but speaks with the tone of a man who has seen plenty of the underside of Japan. Hinode-san is old enough to have seen many of the changing trends in Japan's bar business, and speaks with confidence about the reasons he sees for such places to exist in Japanese society.

"I used to go to bars with girls a lot. Back in my college days, the big thing was *aru saro*, *arubaito* [from German *arbeit*, 'part-time job'] salons. The difference between *arbeit* salons and clubs is that clubs are for members only. In my mind, a club was a place where I didn't have to pay money; the company paid. At *arbeit* salons there was a box where a whole bunch of girls came up, and you chose one. You had to pay a fee for calling a specific girl. It was different depending on the bar, but back in those days the fee was around ¥1,000. Then you had to pay for beer and snacks, so it cost a few thousand yen. After clubs and snacks started becoming more popular, *arbeit* salons started going out of business. In Osaka, near Umeda, there are probably only a couple left. They've gone the way of history, like the cafés. Back in the beginning of the Showa period [1926–89], cafés became popular. They featured dancers in imitation of American and European cafés, and it's where old-time entertainers like Kasagi Shizuko got their start. That was the first time that Japan became Europeanized or Americanized; it's where the modern *mizu shobai* started. The songs that people in their fifties and sixties like, the *kayookyoku*, or folk songs, are all from the cafés.

"After the cafés, cabarets became popular. At a cabaret, you'd talk with girls and dance. Then you could sit in a booth and be close with the girl. When you liked one of the girls, you'd always ask for her the next time, and that was good for her, because she got more money for being called. "

These were places that were affordable for the average Japanese worker. Things are different today. "If a guy isn't an executive, he doesn't have the kind of money for today's top clubs. There are other ways for a guy to have that kind of money, like if he's doing some kind of business on the side. He could be a gangster, make a lot of money in real estate, or he might be a *sookaiya* [stockholder-extortionist, common in Japan]. You might get some stupid son who spends all of the family money. Guys spend amazing amounts of money. Clubs are where all that extra money gets absorbed. It's not necessarily just company entertainment. At really expensive places, if I go with a friend, we might spend ¥200,000 or ¥300,000. One small bottle of Chivas can cost ¥70,000."

Why do Japanese men spend more money to have a drink at a bar or club than they would to have sex at a Turkish bath? "I don't like Turkish baths. I'm sure there are a lot of men who feel the same way. I guess it's a matter of pride. It's embarrassing. It's not shameful to go to a club, but if you go to a Turkish bath, you feel wretched about yourself. You'd be better off to have sex with a blow-up doll."

The Japanese make a clear distinction between paying a professional for sex and having an affair. "A Japanese wife may say, 'You can play with a professional, but don't touch an amateur.' If he gets wrapped up in a real love affair, the family budget gets affected, and the family breaks up. It's like America, with all that divorce. In Japan, people try to live on without getting a divorce. Some Japanese wives would say, 'If you're in Taiwan, it's OK to fool around, but don't do it near home.' It has nothing to do with her family that way.

"From ancient days in Japan, men had many women, even in the Meiji period. They had second and third wives, and it was acknowledged by the first wives. It was a matter of the husband's rank. Even at the end of the Meiji period and the beginning of the Showa period, there were many households where the first and second wives lived together. Even now there are some households like that. It's not typical, but it happens, and sometimes the wives get along very well. That's because the husband is great. He's the boss of the house. They can't complain."

Wives seem to strike a delicate balance between trusting husbands and turning the other way. "Women can choose to trust, or they can doubt their husbands, but 'to doubt is endless'. If she decides to have faith in him, it's easy. If she doesn't trust him, every time he comes home late, she says, 'You're late. You smell like perfume. There's lipstick on your collar.' It's never ending, painful. Japanese women would rather take the easier route, trust. You can trust once and for all or doubt forever. My wife says, 'I'm trusting you, so don't do anything bad!' And then I tell her, 'Of course not!'"

What's the percentage of Japanese men who fool around? "It depends on where you draw the line of being unfaithful. Is going to a bar and talking with a hostess that you like being unfaithful, or is it only when you go to a hotel with a woman? Maybe you go to a bar with a friend, and tell him how cute you think one of the girls is, and then he goes and tells everyone you're fooling around—even though you've never touched her. Some think it's infidelity if you just like a girl, others if you have sex, and others even if you simply spend time with a girl. If you draw the line at having sex, there really aren't that many unfaithful men. I don't know the real percentages, but even if one out of ten men goes that far, it's not that all of them are real playboys. Some have just stumbled into an affair. There are all sorts."

Hinode-san's speech about wives who trust their husbands notwithstanding, he admits that it's not easy if an affair is found out. "In Japan, wives are the property of their husbands, so there is one character in the home. If one person does something destructive, it destroys the whole family. So if an affair happens, the wife feels insulted, and that's like insulting yourself, since you're one character together. It's that way of thinking that won't let wives forgive."

Hinode-san confirms what Nakano-san said about the product being sold in the *mizu shobai*. "The bar and club business isn't selling alcohol, they're selling something invisible: charm, flattery, a feeling, an atmosphere. There are certain taboos in the club world, and one of them is the question, 'How much is this?' You can't ask how much something costs, whether it's the drink, or how much it is for a girl to sit next to you. In the sex industry specifically, you can ask how much it is for one time with a girl, but in the club world, they're selling something you can't quantify. You can't ask how much the atmosphere costs, just as you can't ask the price of the beer. You know it should be a ¥500 beer, but you're probably going to pay ¥2,000."

There are benefits to spending time at clubs. "If you insult your wife, she'll argue with you. If you insult a hostess at a club or snack, she won't argue. Some girls take a lot of abuse." During a different conversation when Hinode-san had been drinking, he expressed some strong feelings. "Women at those places are like dogs. You can kick a dog, and yell at it, and it can't do anything to you. It's a way to let off stress. That's what they're there for." He backed away from that statement to a degree when he was sober. "I don't feel sorry for the girls who join the business voluntarily; they're in there by their own choice. I feel bad for girls who are forced to work in the *mizu shobai*, though. There are places like Tobita [one of the old prostitution districts of Osaka], where women still work in brothels surrounded by Edo-period walls built to keep girls from escaping. It was very common for impoverished families to sell their daughters; those girls were a kind of human mortgage."

As Hinode-san spoke about Tobita, I recalled my own visit to that "historic" area. While living in Japan, I had heard a rumor that the remains of the fifteen-foot walls that enclosed Tobita could still be seen. I was determined to go there so that I could look around and get a feel for the atmosphere. Shinsekai and Tsutenkaku, the once booming entertainment and amusement areas near Tobita, are now filled with cheap porn movie theaters, strip joints, *pachinko* (Japanese pinball-like game) parlors, and the rumpled belongings of the countless vagrants who live in the area.

Having been warned that these down-and-out districts, particularly the walled-in area of Tobita, were not safe places for a young woman to walk alone, I went with a male escort during daylight hours. With no makeup, short hair, and baggy men's clothes, I walked down the steps into a sunken area surrounded by stone walls. Sure enough, the walls were still there, now without the guards who had made sure no woman escaped.

This was not just a prostitution district of the past; the trade was still actively being plied as we walked. Hiding my face behind the umbrella that was also keeping off a light drizzle, I walked through the streets of Tobita with my escort. The *yaritebaba* (older women who act as pimpsprocuresses) that I thought had disappeared long ago sat in the open doorway of each house, waving and calling to us as we walked by. "*Oniisan*, young man, come in! It's cheap! Welcome!" A younger, but not necessarily young woman kneeled quietly on a cushion next to each older woman, looking out at us or down at the floor. I tried hard to see as much as possible without showing my face, which would reveal that I was not only a woman but a foreigner.

Behind the women in the doorway there was usually a bouncer who encouraged customers to get their business over with as quickly as possible. Speed being of the essence, most of the prostitutes wore loose skirts and no underwear. Hoping to get photographs of the area but not wanting to get caught doing so, I hid my camera under my jacket and aimed the lens through a hole. Unfortunately, since I was unable to focus or aim well, the photos are of very poor quality. But I can attest to the fact that the walls certainly do exist, and so do the descendants of their unfortunate occupants. Today it is not the walls that hold these women in, but usually the threat of beatings or the promise of drugs.

Hinode-san doesn't see any permanent slowdown in the drinking and hostess businesses of Japan. "*Mizu shobai* places will stay around. People in Japan don't have anything else to do. Rich people in Europe or America are also rich in free time, free to do the things they want. The Japanese don't have hobbies or interests to occupy themselves, so they look for a place to spend their money. An American might buy a yacht, go to resorts, buy a nice camera or play various sports, but the Japanese work so much they throw away their interests and forget them.

"Sure, there are guys who like to golf or surf, but there are no studious hobbies where you can get seriously involved. Oh, everybody has a piano in the house, but they don't have real knowledge or interest in music, they just order their kids to learn to play the piano. In Europe, in one house there will be a flute, in another a guitar, in another an oboe. Everyone has his own interests.

"Since the Japanese don't have their own interests, they rush to whatever the latest trend is. Everyone has to say, 'This is my hobby.' Any new fad becomes a national pastime. There might be one out of a hundred people with a sincere interest in something, but most people know only how to *talk* about a hobby, they don't do it. These people don't want to go home because they don't have anything to say to their wives; and the only thing they ever read is about their jobs. So they go out drinking at *mizu shobai* places. This is Japan's fate. Even in America, people with no special interests spend their free time out drinking at bars, don't they? It's the same anywhere.

"The kind of place where it's taboo to ask, 'How much does this cost?' won't disappear from Japan until everyone becomes rich enough in free time to develop some kind of hobby or activity. When the average Japanese comes to that point, these places might disappear, but not until then."

KUWADA-SAN AND SAITO-SAN

Bar and club customers can spend large sums of money in an evening, but nowhere can the subtle extravagance of an *ochaya*, a geisha teahouse, be matched. Treated to an evening of entertainment at one of Gion's fine geisha houses for the purpose of conducting an interview, I devoured half a plate of *fugu* sashimi, thin slices of raw blowfish famous for the deadly poison it holds. This delicacy can be legally prepared only by certified chefs, a law justified by the number of deaths each year of customers who eat parts of the fish tainted by the poison it carries. I later found out that the blowfish alone cost the equivalent of $200 to $300. The many other delicacies and fine sakè flavored with dried *fugu* tails and fins were only a fraction of the cost of the evening's entertainment. Kuwada-san, a successful lawyer, and Saito-san, a wealthy landowner and company president, offered this evening to me to learn about the upper echelons of the *mizu shobai* world. Their comments were interspersed with those of the charming *okami-san*, the proprietress of the teahouse. The more than five hours we spent enjoying the offerings of the geisha world no doubt cost my hosts the equivalent of many hundreds of dollars.

"This is the ultimate kind of place for Japanese men," Kuwada-san says. "It's extravagant, and it seems expensive, which is why they long to come here. The truth is, however, that an *ochaya* is cheaper than going to some of the bars. Even if a man wants to come to this kind of place, he usually can't because he doesn't know a place to go. He can be introduced only by a man who is already a customer in the *ochaya*. If I introduced you here and you came in and ordered lots of drinks and food and didn't pay, I would have to pay for all of it. The system is for protection. You don't introduce anyone you don't trust."

The conversation turns to the importance of selecting a particular drinking establishment as the site for doing business. In fact, most men come to teahouses for company business entertainment. Saito-san gives an example. "It's tax time, and I call up someone I know in the tax department and ask him to get together with me for a drink. If he comes, I know my tax situation is OK. There are subtleties in terms of choosing the right kind of place to meet and have a drink. For example, if I come to this *ochaya*, I know that no matter what is said in this room, it will never leak out. I know I can trust this house completely, no matter what the conversation." The *okami-san* adds, "I may have a customer here tonight with one set of guests, and then he comes in again tomorrow night. I won't say anything about the previous evening, won't even refer to it if he doesn't. I operate as if that evening never existed."

Saito-san continues, "It takes a special kind of sensitivity to run a place like this. The people who come here are from positions of great responsibility. That puts a lot of pressure on the *okami-san* to make everything run smoothly. For example, if she makes one wrong move or says one wrong thing to ruin the atmosphere during those few seconds of actual business talk, the whole deal could be shot. You don't find the kind of sensitivity and trust in bar hostesses that you do in geisha in a teahouse like this."

"That's why you have to be so careful about the place you choose to invite someone," says Kuwada-san. You can't just say to yourself, 'It's a teahouse, so it's OK,' or, 'If there are girls, any place is OK'. People bring their important guests only to a place they're absolutely sure about. That's what makes an *ochaya* like this worth the price—that trust."

Exactly what kind of business goes on in the teahouse? Kuwada-san explains that discussions never include contract details. "The business that occurs in this environment is very simple. It's only whether a deal will go forward or not. That's all. No negotiations, no prices. That's decided before or after drinking. You have to understand that out of three hours of being in this *ochaya*, only ten seconds are spent actually discussing business. I can come in and spend hours talking about the weather, sports or whatever with a business associate. It's only when I get up to leave that I briefly say, 'Oh, best regards on that business deal.' That's the Japanese way of doing business.

"The worst thing anyone could ever do is to sit down in a place like this and pull out a bunch of documents and start talking prices. That would be like Japan and Russia trying to negotiate something. There are ten or twenty preliminary meetings, and at the very last one, the Minister of Foreign Affairs comes in and signs a pact. That's the kind of place this is, where the final OK is stamped. It's a ritual, a ceremony. Individuals like us coming in for pleasure is unusual; it's almost all business-related at these places. Top guys come in here, they drink and talk, and when they leave, you know the deal is on."

Saito-san brings up the topic of traditional seating arrangements at the *ochaya*. "There's a difference between the Japanese style and Chinese style of seating rank. The Chinese have a diagonal pattern. Here, the person being entertained sits away from the door, while the entertaining party sits near the door. The most important person sits in the middle. To his right sits his *migi ude,* or number-two man."

Underlying motives for men spending their time and money in places like the *ochaya* emerge as Kuwada-san and Saito-san start to feel the effects of the sakè. "Gion has its own special culture. To put it simply, these places exist because men commit adultery. If there were no one but men here, no one would come." The *okami-san* adds, "It is a mixture. If men came here for nothing but pure business, there would be no excitement in coming here, no reason to call a *maiko* or *geiko* in to dance and entertain."

How onerous are the financial demands of being an official patron, the *danna-san*, of a geisha? "Even the president of a huge Japanese company would have trouble becoming a geisha's *danna-san*," according to Saito-san. "A man would have to be the owner of his own business to have that kind of money."

Kuwada-san elaborates on the geisha-patron connection. "In the old days of Kyoto, there was a saying, 'Never cross a white *tabi*.' This means don't get mixed up with someone wearing white *tabi*, or there will be trouble. This refers both to Kyoto's monks and the geisha of the *iromachi* ['color town', or sex district]. You don't know what powerful person they might be connected with, and you could really get hurt. Even the *okami-san* here, though she doesn't say it, knows people you can't imagine, people in very high places. If we did something bad to her, we might be sorry.

"It would be really interesting for you to see where the money behind geisha and *maiko* comes from. That information alone would make a great book." As customers, Kuwada-san and Saito-san are also part of the money behind the geisha and *maiko*. "Tonight, there will be a number of geisha and *maiko* coming in. With all of the evening's expenses totalled, we'll probably have to pay ¥100,000 each for this evening. This is a special evening, but normally, one of us would have to pay ¥20,000 or ¥30,000."

But the prestige to be gained by associating with geisha is worth the high tariff. "If people find out a man's fooling around with a hostess, they think he's a jerk," says Saito-san. "If they find out he's having an affair with a geisha, they look at him in awe. Recently, a high-ranking securities executive was found to be having an affair with a famous actress. That didn't look good. But if his lover were a geisha, he would have looked great. This is tradition. It won't change."

Kuwada adds, "In their hearts, this is where Japanese men want to be able to come. An *ochaya* is the ultimate, image-wise. If a friend asks another friend, 'What's Suzuki-san been doing lately?', and the friend says he's been hanging out at a snack or bar, he'll say, 'What the hell is he doing?' Bars and snacks don't have a good image. But if the friend is told that Suzuki-san has been frequenting a Gion teahouse, that will earn him a great deal of respect."

What are Saito-san's motives for frequenting the elite teahouses? "I come here for the atmosphere, for the spirit of dignity and grace. The difference in quality and mood changes the taste of the whiskey. It tastes good here because of the *okami-san* running it, because of the level of atmosphere maintained here."

Kuwada-san adds, "Sure, there are occasions when it's more appropriate to take a client to a bar than to a teahouse, but while you might have a Japanese man who complains about going to a bar, no one would complain about coming to a teahouse. He can sit here and not drink at all and still have a good time. Places like this are expensive because they take the trouble to have fine things around. Look at this cup, or the vase over there. They are some of the best pottery you can find, and they are expensive, but subtly placed here as if it was no big deal. If a customer isn't sensitive to these things, if he can't spot a fine piece of work and appreciate the fact that it is here in the room he is being served in, then there's no reason for him to spend the money to be in a teahouse."

The *okami-san* turns the subject to the traditions and ceremonies that dictate geisha life. "When a *geiko* makes her debut, she goes from teahouse to teahouse accompanied by a man, greeting all the other geisha and teahouse people. She wears a formal black kimono marked with her family crest for the first three days, and for the next three days she wears a formal kimono of bright, cheerful colors. As time goes on, if she gets a *danna-san* [many geisha don't], there is another ceremony, the geisha district's own wedding ceremony, where all of the geisha and *okami-san* come to recognize the match. The restaurants contribute some *sekihan* [red bean rice prepared for celebrations]. Then the couple distributes red and white bean cakes around the geisha district. Of course he has a legal wife and family somewhere, but this is his Gion family." The geisha's rank changes according to the rank of her *danna-san*.

Saito-san gives another perspective on the geisha-patron relationship. "After this geisha district marriage, the geisha is his property. If he has a lot of money, he'll build her a teahouse; if he doesn't have that much, he'll buy her a nice condo. But a *danna-san* doesn't come around all that often. As he gets older, to be frank, their sex life isn't good—he can't perform well sexually. At some point, she wants to fool around on him, but he hires a man to control her. It ends up being controlled prostitution. But there's a long history and high cultural level involved, so there's still awe for the geisha."

Saito-san and Kuwada-san admit that their wives are neglected because of their nocturnal activities. "In America that would be grounds for divorce, wouldn't it?," Kuwada-san says laughingly. "Japanese men are terrible, aren't they? But being here is like being in your own home. It's comfortable. The difference is that here the women always have makeup on, whereas a real wife doesn't. This is home with makeup. Having affairs seems to have been an accepted practice in Japan for years, but it really isn't accepted under the surface. Japanese men love their wives—they just love them in a different way from

American men. There's a saying that a good wife is like air—she's necessary for life, but you don't see or feel her.

"Wives expect their husbands to sleep with them. It's a husband's duty. Sometimes things happen, though. There's your wife, waiting for you, and suddenly a friend from out of town calls and asks to get together to drink right now. You have to choose your wife or the friend. Your wife will be there for years to come. In Japanese society, you can't choose your wife in this case. That would be the end of everything."

Chapter Six

OUTSIDERS:
TOKEN WHITES

When I started working at Club Regent, I was the only Westerner there, but halfway through my stay, a blonde bombshell named Hilde, from Sweden, came on board. I spoke Japanese; she spoke none. I made an attempt to get along with the staff; she ignored them. I didn't complain about things; Hilde complained frequently. I followed what I had observed as the rules of the club as well as I could, trying to fit in and not make waves. She drank too much, got out of control, and spoke sharply to the customers. I fit in almost too well for a foreigner. Hilde stuck out like a sore thumb, not only because of her tall, buxom build and blonde hair, but because of her sometimes outrageous actions. I lost my job. She was hired whenever she came back to Japan from Europe on a tourist visa, and invited to stay as long as she liked. Hilde was the perfect token white hostess, providing stark contrast to the Japanese and other Asian hostesses, a novelty that brought customers in and kept them there out of curiosity.

There are thousands of non-Japanese, including hundreds of Western women, who willingly work in Japan's nightclub and sex trade. In contrast with the sometimes subtle, indirect answers of Japanese interviewees, Western *mizu shobai* workers tend to be quite frank in their views. An American, Australian, and Canadian hostess offer glimpses of their personal experiences in Tokyo and Kyoto bars as well as their views of the hostessing business.

CARRIE

Tall and slender, Carrie has a mellifluous voice that veils the powerful punch of her words. An American photojournalist, Carrie was drawn to the *mizu shobai* for the same reason most women are: the money. "I had been in Japan for a year or so, teaching English and making a fairly good wage, but I wanted money to travel, so I figured, what the hell, I'll try hostessing. I worked at Club Celine for three or four months, and it had to be one of the most frustrating experiences I've ever had. Celine wasn't terribly expensive, and a lot of salarymen, not executives, went there. They were men in their forties and fifties who hadn't travelled much—local Kyoto and Osaka people. Although there were some shy, pleasant men who were fairly easy to talk to, there were also men who were basically insecure and had a foreigner complex. The only way they knew how to deal with foreign women was to be abusive."

Carrie found certain patterns repeated among the customers of Club Celine. "What really freaked me out about some of these customers was how incredibly rude they were. I was regularly asked, 'What color is your pubic hair? Is it the same color as your hair on your head?' 'How tall are you?' 'How big are your tits?' 'Have you slept with Japanese men? They're smaller than foreign men, aren't they?' I thought, maybe this is normal, they're just not uptight about these things, and I got pretty good at dodging their questions and laughing. It was pointless to get offended, because you get hurt, and they get hurt. Rarely would I fail to strike up a reasonably interesting conversation, although occasionally I just couldn't."

Maintaining good relations with customers is only one aspect of the foreign hostess's challenge. She must also get along with coworkers in a not always friendly environment. "The girls at that club were all decent to the foreign girls, but they seemed to look at me and think, 'You're just an amateur . . . you're just here for a little while . . . you're a foreigner.' There was absolutely no relationship that could be developed. I wasn't a threat to them and they weren't a threat to me, so we maintained an even keel. But the mama in Celine did a weird thing to me one time, which showed me her true feelings about foreigners, and about Americans, especially.

"One night she was really drunk and as I was about to leave, she started screaming at me, 'You Americans, you think you can do anything you want, you think you can rule the world! I hate Americans!' I was just standing there, and the other customers didn't get involved, they just watched. I'd only planned to be at the club for a few more weeks, and I really wanted the money, so I just thought, 'OK, forget it,' and went home. The Japanese are good about hiding it, but I'm convinced they really hate Americans, in many ways. There's still a tremendous amount of animosity left in the people who were involved in the war, people in their sixties and seventies."

No hostess, Japanese or other, has escaped unpleasant experiences in clubs. But the opportunity for outsiders to see a hidden side of Japan is a special chance many find worth the trauma. "I learned things about Japan that I wouldn't have learned otherwise. I saw a very ugly, unattractive side, and it really turned me off. Some nights I just felt like throwing up; I didn't know how to handle it. The Japanese girls are really very clever in dealing with the men. They know how to put them in their places. There was also a language barrier for me, of course. I couldn't give it back to them in tough language. It's not easy keeping those guys happy."

Like many other foreigners in the *mizu shobai*, Carrie found that the financial benefits made up for the distasteful scenes. "After working at Celine, I travelled and went back to the States for about a year and a half, then I came back and was totally broke again. A friend introduced me to a woman she'd known for thirty years, the owner of a club called Cheri, just a few doors down from Celine. This woman was so interesting. Where the mama-san at Celine is kind of crude, middle-class, probably slept with the customers a lot, the mama-san at Cheri is high-class, the antithesis of Celine's mama. She's older, maybe late fifties or early sixties, but very well preserved. She's not married, but she obviously has a patron-lover. I don't know who he is, but he's a really high-level businessman or politician, and of course he's married and has his own family and his own life.

"She doesn't run Cheri for money, but for fun, and she's been losing customers because she's been losing interest in the club. You have to keep relations with these guys by calling them up at their office and saying, 'Oh, come by, I haven't seen you in a long time.' I'm sure she hasn't been doing that, so slowly but surely, people have stopped coming. I love the lady. She's simple but smart."

At Cheri, Carrie started to understand more about Japanese clubs and how a foreigner relates to that environment. "I worked at Cheri for only a month. The girls there were much more upper crust; it was a whole different scene. This mama loved pink, and the whole damn place was turned into a little pink palace. I was so out of place in the funky, cheap clothes that I'd borrowed from my hostess friend. It was amazing that there were even a couple of girls there who were nice to me, because these hostesses are truly professional. More often than not they would ignore me. I think I was the first and last foreigner that mama has ever hired, so the girls didn't quite know how to deal with me. The customers at Cheri were a bit classier, a little more genteel and easier to deal with. Nobody ever tried to grab me because I'm so tall, even taller than the men. I always got the questions, though—'How tall are you? How old are you? Where are you from?'—and it's one of the things that drove me nuts.

"I quit Cheri because I had decided to move to Tokyo. When I'd started, I told the mama-san that I was only going to be there for one month. At first she was iffy about it, but I think in the end she appreciated my honesty. I was also introduced by her friend, which is very important in Japan. I didn't realize how much the Japanese talk behind your back: They want to know your exact story, precisely what your position is. People would ask the mama how she knew me, and when she would say I was introduced through a friend, that made it OK. I've kept in touch. I'd like to maintain a relationship with her."

When Carrie moved to Tokyo, money was still a problem. "I was broke; we're talking only ¥200 in my pocket. I knew I had to hostess again, since I didn't have enough other work yet to cover my expenses. The people I was staying with knew an influential man who owned a lot of clubs in Tokyo, and he introduced me to a mama who said she might be interested in having a foreigner as a hostess."

Being physically different from Japanese women was always an issue for Carrie. "It was a tiny club, and when I walked in I thought, I can't work in this place, I'm too big! The mama took me to a coffee shop and told me how much she was going to pay me—¥13,000 a night. There wasn't much difference between my Kyoto and Tokyo pay. The girls get paid at all different levels, but it was something no one ever talked about directly."

Despite a certain degree of strictness in her new mama-san's expectations, Carrie found she could respect her. "She's an amazing woman, one of these workhorse types who has never had a patron. She worked as a hostess for twelve years and probably got shit about her age at the end. She finally scraped up enough savings and borrowed money from some of her better customers to put a down payment on her own place in Ginza. Many of the girls left her club because she was strict, telling them what to wear, what to say to the customers, what they could and couldn't do. She never bothered me, though, because I'm a foreigner, which puts me on a different level. To me, she is *the* struggling Japanese woman, *the* liberated businesswoman of Japan. I admire her for working so hard. I don't think she's a lesbian, but a lot of these women are. I had no idea when I first came here, but there's a tremendous amount of bisexuality and homosexuality in Japan. It's more visible and intense in Tokyo than in other parts of Japan."

The Tokyo mama does well business-wise, but is she satisfied with her accomplishments? "Do I think she's happy? That's a good question. I've always wondered that. I don't think she really knows what happiness is. This is her lot, her life, and she's doing well, even though her parents probably had no money and she has no patron, which is almost unheard of. Almost all of these women have a man behind the scenes."

Like many other Japanese and foreign hostesses, Carrie had other work besides the nightclub. "When I started working at the club in

Tokyo I was going in about four nights a week, and then cut it down to two. I fluctuated back and forth. Sometimes it was because I couldn't handle the whole scene, but eventually I just got too busy with my other work.

"I was working an incredible schedule. I'd get up in the morning at 7:00 or 8:00, write letters or take photographs, drop by my old office, hang out and try to do a few things. I'd be running all day, riding ten subways back to back every day. I'd hurry to my English class, which started around 4:30 in the afternoon, being late more often than not, and teach until about 7:00. Then I'd quickly take the subway to the Ginza area, change my clothes and put my makeup on in the public toilet. I'd rush over to the club, get there about 8:00, work until about 11:45, and then catch the last train home, totally exhausted. It was insane."

There was always a danger of being "found out" as a part of the *mizu shobai* world. "In Tokyo, most of the people I know are professionals in photography. I couldn't tell any of them, or writers or reporters, that I was working as a hostess. It's such a small professional community that it would have eventually gotten back to the news agency I was working for. If they found out that I was hostessing, it would be embarrassing, it would be just awful. I had a photojournalist visa, and it was illegal for me to be working as a hostess."

The attitudes Carrie had found among Kyoto customers didn't seem as prevalent in Tokyo. "The difference was like night and day. There's one episode that kind of says it all. I'd been working at the club in Tokyo for almost two years. One night I was sitting with a group of men whom I knew fairly well and was comfortable with. We were chatting, and they got drunker and drunker. One guy finally said to me in Japanese, 'Is your pubic hair the same color as the hair on your head?' It blew me away because I hadn't heard that in a long time—not since I was in

Kyoto. No one had ever been that rude at this club in Tokyo. I looked at him and said in Japanese, 'I haven't been asked that in a long time. Where are you from? Kyoto?' I wasn't surprised when he said, 'Yes.'

"But in general, the customers at the Tokyo club were a reflection of the mama's personality. She had known these guys for twenty years. She was a true mama-san in that she knew about their wives, their problems, their families. They'd come by the club or wherever she was to see her, even if only once a year. Guys from one company often frequent the same club in groups. When I was there she had competing companies as customers, and it was really tense. They'll be pleasant to each other to a point, but they really are enemies. She was playing too many cards, so to speak. I know one man who doesn't go to her club anymore because it was so embarrassing for him to meet his rivals."

Carrie saw the down side of what can be a very lucrative business. "Her club is not terribly expensive, about the same as Celine. One person would be charged about ¥10,000 to ¥15,000, plus the bottle. No cash was exchanged for regular customers; the mama would send bills to the office. A couple of times she had guys who wouldn't pay at all, and she finally had to tell them to leave and not come back. There are a lot of crooks, people who seem to be very nice who are actually just ripoff artists. She had to be very careful about that. It's a tough business.

"I only worked at that one club in Tokyo, and I met some really nice men there. In fact, one of them is now one of my best photography clients. About half the customers spoke English really well, and a lot of them had lived abroad with their families. Since Tokyo is the business center of Japan, most of the really top-level executives are there, so it seems to be a whole different breed of people, much more cosmopolitan. I often had full evenings of English conversation with these guys. There was a difference in the people there, but there was also a difference in me. I was more confident and more comfortable, so I knew how to handle them better."

The strain of long, late hours as well as cultural differences took their toll on Carrie. "I didn't drink at all in the club, because I was so weak and tired. The mama understood that, but it made the customers uncomfortable, because there's nothing worse than an uptight hostess. Toward the end I got so sick of the whole damn thing that I wouldn't laugh, or I'd get a little bitchy, and that's just the worst. The customers don't need that, and they don't want it."

After years of floating in and out of Japan's nightclub scene, Carrie left. "I finally quit not just because of all of my photography work but because hostessing is a hard job. It's tiring. It's humiliating. Even though in Tokyo I had nice conversations with people, it's still just mindless talk. The language barrier was a factor. I was completely left out of some conversations that had people rolling on the floor. If I could have understood, it would have been more entertaining. More than anything, the boredom got to me, I'm sure. I told the mama a month ahead of time that I was going to the States for a couple of months and that I probably wouldn't be coming back to work for her."

There were aftereffects from leaving the club, both financial and emotional. "It was a great feeling of freedom for a while after I quit, but then I had a lot of pressures. Money was pretty tight for awhile, and I'd also quit my English teaching at the same time, but I got by OK. I remember the feeling in Kyoto of just hating the customers and thinking what pigs they are, and that feeling has mellowed since I've been away from hostessing awhile."

Distance and time to reflect changed Carrie's perspective on and understanding of the *mizu shobai* scene. "I made the Kyoto men sound really awful; they're really not that bad. If anything, it's sad. It's the only way that they can let off steam. The hostess has to be a sounding board, and she knows it. She ends up being psychiatrist, mother, daughter, lover, doctor. It's very important, this hostess thing. Without it, business in Japan couldn't exist. It's very interesting, too, to see the relationships between the men, how they act if the *shachoo* [president] comes, all the different hierarchical levels. It's interesting to observe who holds court. You have to laugh at the boss's jokes; the club always gives the prettiest hostess to the boss. To a foreigner working in a hostess club, it seems like a very superficial world—people are inconsiderate, drunk, and brutish—but there's so much more to it than that.

"The clubs are really an integral part of the whole Japanese social scene. The Japanese understand the relationships and know how to deal with them. They know what's good and bad within that world. It's the foreigners who don't understand the relationships, don't know how to deal with it all and get offended. It's just so foreign to us. Yet it's really right out there on the plate, right there in front of our faces, more than probably any other relationship. It's a real eye-opener. It seems like a really ugly side of Japan, but if you get behind it, it's not so ugly. It's an important part of the culture, and it works."

DEBBIE

Debbie has short fair hair, wears almost no makeup, and is serious, but easygoing. From Hobart, Tasmania, she came to Japan with far less exposure to big-city life than fellow Australians from cities like Sydney. Nevertheless, she has spent more time in Japan's club world than most other foreigners, giving her not only a more in-depth view than many, but also a reputation among the foreign women as the local hostess club expert.

Debbie had heard about the lucrative aspect of working at Japanese bars before she left Australia. "I had a girlfriend in Tasmania who'd worked as a hostess in Japan about ten years ago. The money at that time was ¥5,000 an hour or more. I had no idea how to go about getting this work. I had this really gutsy Australian girlfriend who came across and did it. I refused to work for English schools, so the only other opportunity I had was to join my girlfriend."

Debbie and her friend plunged headfirst into the bar world of Kyoto. "We didn't speak a word of Japanese, but we got jobs working in this *yakuza* club called Cosmo. We were the only Western women there." Not all clubs have *yakuza* clientele, and many hostesses never have to deal with them. At Cosmo, however, Debbie saw her fair share. "You can tell by the aura of the *yakuza* guys that they have power. If they want something they'll get it. It was an incredible experience. I worked there for over a year without realizing what I was into. There were guys coming in with fingers missing and lots of bodyguards around. I knew we were in a sticky situation, but I didn't realize the kind of things that could have happened. My girlfriend was roughed up a bit—they pushed you off your chair sometimes in this particular club, though that doesn't happen in most clubs. It also upset me that the Cosmo customers were really into touching the women. When I first started there, a man pushed me off my seat onto the floor and tried to slip a banana up my dress. I was scared to death. I finally just got up and left, moved to another table. No one tried to help me, but they would in the place I'm in now."

Nonetheless, not all of Debbie's *yakuza* encounters were bad. "Actually, some of the *yakuza* groups would come in with their families. I'd relax a little more when there were groups like that." Sometimes the *yakuza* customers are nicer than "upstanding citizens" who frequent clubs. "The mama at Cosmo told me that the wealthy, middle-aged bankers were the worst when it came to being lecherous."

The high wages that Debbie had heard about ten years earlier had decreased, a result of supply and demand. "The pay was ¥3,000 an hour. I get paid the same now. The Western women who have since joined my current club are getting only ¥2,500." At Cosmo, Debbie and her girlfriend had to adjust to unfamiliar surroundings. "Every night at Cosmo was bizarre. They had these atrocious strip shows, and if there were no customers we had to go to the front and applaud so the performers thought there were customers. There was a lot of prostitution going on, too. I was so naive at the time, it was all happening right in front of me and it just didn't click.

"I got thrown out of Cosmo. I don't know why; maybe I didn't dress well enough. The women wore kimono or full dresses every night. I'd always wonder where the young girls got the money. I couldn't understand any Japanese, but I could follow the process of a pick-up and a 'Yes, I'll meet you. . . .' They're all incredible women, real gutsy ladies. I still see some of them around, working at different places. They see me and call me Anna because that was my name at Cosmo. I use my real name now."

Although Debbie had to leave the club, her friend didn't. "She was very attractive, and I think they preferred her being there to me. They kept her there, and her character changed a lot; she even started going out with some of the customers, which I've always refused to do. She was talking about being a mama-san and stuff like that. I changed, too, but for the better, I think. I'm so patient now, especially with men and their ways. I've also learned all these devious ways of weaving around dirty talk and stray questions I get asked. You learn how to listen to people, and you learn how to sit straight.

"After Cosmo, I went out by myself looking for a hostessing job, and within six months I had worked in three little bars. Then I found a place called Mimi. It was the only place where I cried because of the way I was treated. Your soul has to be pretty hard out there. They'd just throw you out if another, better-looking person came along. At Mimi, they just fired me flat out, and that was my only job, I didn't have anything else. It took some effort to pick myself up and go back out looking again, and I didn't have any money for about two weeks. At the club I'm working in now, my mama is so different. She'll just drag on to the end, even if she's got someone working who's not so good. She hasn't had the heart to ask anyone to leave, but eventually she has to."

Kind-hearted mamas get good reviews from their workers, but they don't often do as well in business. "I've been watching over the years, and I can see that Mama is worried about business. She even re-\decorated the whole place in the latest trendy style, but it hasn't picked up a great deal. In addition to the economic pressures, there have been a lot of restrictions on bars recently. All these instructions, hundreds of things you can't do." These government controls have affected *mizu shobai* incomes, but general economic trends have had a more far reaching effect than these rules.

"Hostesses who have their own sets of regular customers that they bring in help keep clubs busy. Maybe that's another reason why my friend did better at Cosmo than I did. She went out with the customers and then brought them into the club with her. I wouldn't play that game, I just never could. I also had my suspicions that she was actually letting other things happen when she was out with these guys, but I really didn't know. That was another thing that put a strain on our friendship. I just didn't know the other side of her. The clubs can do that to you."

Debbie's current club is on the small side. "The club holds about forty customers. Sometimes we've had big groups in, even groups of Americans connected with some Japanese company. That's great fun. Everyone just goes wild. The Japanese hostesses don't know how to handle Americans' different manners—standing up at the bar or putting their feet up—so it's funny to watch their faces. They enjoy it, though. When I have really favorite customers, I let everything go and almost forget that I'm working.

"I feel comfortable there, and I'm really close to the Japanese women. Hostesses at many clubs are real professionals, but the women at this club aren't. They all work full-time jobs during the day. One works in the post office, another works for a bank, and the other is a kimono maker. None of them is married. They're all about my age, twenty-nine, but they think they're old. One woman has just met a man and is wondering if she'll be able to marry him because she's too old!"

As Carrie described, not only the character of the hostesses and mama changes from club to club, but so does the character of the customers. "If there's a friend of a friend of a friend who's brought into the club, and he's rude, the repercussions go back to the person at the beginning, and that keeps a really good balance to the place. I like nearly all of our customers. We have gardeners, professors, doctors, gas company men, regular businessmen—all kinds of people. There's one customer who's both a brother and father for me. He's mid-forties, married with children. He's in hospital right now, so I've been going there quite a lot to see him. He's the first person I've ever gone someplace outside the club with, though never alone. He's an architect, and he's unusual in that he just packs up his work stuff and takes off to Nepal for awhile, which is very unusual for the Japanese. He calls these trips 'company sabotage.' He just gets up and goes."

It is often difficult for foreigners to have good relationships with club staff because of the attitude toward foreigners as expendable objects. In fact, Debbie gets along quite well with her current mama despite occasional problems, one of which is that Debbie likes to speak Japanese with her customers, and speaks it well. "The mama has been getting onto me about that. Customers don't like it when the Japanese gets beyond the cute stage. I'll have to talk with her about that. I don't like taking orders from anyone, and she knows that. She needs me there, I'm sort of valuable to her, so I can say those things to her. She could get rid of me any time she wants, of course, but I've been there so long that if I wasn't there, people would be asking, 'Where's Debbie? Why isn't she here?'"

Like Carrie, Debbie's daytime schedule conflicted with her night job, and she's gradually been cutting down on the number of hours she works at the club. "I just couldn't cope with working that much any more because I was also studying Japanese in the mornings. The club is officially open only until 1:00, but they usually don't dump everyone out until 2:00 or 3:00. I only work until midnight. The mama wanted me to work a lot later, but I put my foot down. I work only two nights a week now. I also teach English—only private lessons for people I like—and I model for art schools. I'm my own boss in all my work now, and I don't have anybody keeping me under their thumb. No one can take all my income away from me at once. I don't sign contracts; I'm a free agent; and I don't trust anyone."

After having spent years as a hostess, Debbie has had time to think about how it fits into her life. "It used to really depress me to think, 'Is this my profession in life, to work in a place like this?' I felt self-conscious about not using my mind and my abilities, but now I think working as a hostess is important for me. I think I know a lot more about

Japanese than a lot of other foreigners, and I've also learned a lot about the history of Japan."

Not everything has been positive. "I have a Japanese boyfriend, and he doesn't like me working there and getting upset when people abuse me. He reacts very strongly when a Japanese will point at me in the street or on a train and loudly call out '*gaijin! gaijin!*' While he's concerned about me, he has also said recently that he can see that working at the club has helped me a lot. I think I understand more about Japan and its people than he does sometimes. I have more patience with people and the things they do.

"I'm in the business of selling whiskey, but it sort of scares me what alcohol and alcoholism do to people. I don't drink much; I always get by on a weak drink while I work." As they were for Carrie, club clothes are an issue, but Debbie's current club is not particularly strict. "I try to buy clothes that I can wear teaching as well as at the club. They always pay me on time at this club, and I don't even keep track of my days anymore, I trust them so much.

"I can honestly say that I enjoy the work now. I don't even think about it when I go. I just put on the makeup, the clothes, and fifteen minutes later I'm there. It's like home, like my own lounge room, and I get paid for it. When I was at Cosmo, everything was completely out of control. I was a night person; I'd sleep all day. Now it's so different."

KAREN

Karen, whose large, bright eyes flash from behind her glasses, is an outspoken Canadian from Vancouver who did numerous short stints at a variety of clubs, primarily in Tokyo. "When I first moved to Japan,

Tokyo was much too big, too fast, too soon, so I came to Kyoto. It didn't seem like some pearl of the Orient. I found an office job at a small trading company in Umeda. It was awful, with nothing to do all day, but the pay was OK. After about six months I decided to split. I moved up to Sado Island and lived with the drumming group called Kodo. It was terrible. I wanted to learn dance, but they lied to me; they didn't have any teacher for dancing.

"I ended up going to Tokyo. I met a German girl and an American girl in the Tokyo Women's International Network, this sort of feminist group. I started asking them about jobs. The German girl said she was a hostess—she said you get paid to sit around and chat and drink. She sent me to a place in Akasaka to have an interview, and they hired me. The pay there was only ¥2,500 an hour, and in 1983, that was really low. The mama was sort of nasty, and used people to get what she wanted. The majority of people working there were foreigners, and since it was near the Akasaka Prince Hotel, Akasaka Tokyu, and other big hotels, there were a lot of foreign customers, too."

It didn't take Karen long to realize that getting hostessing work was not difficult. "The job in Akasaka didn't last very long. The mama was a real bag and I didn't like the pay, so I left. I realized that I was marketable, so I went from bar to bar in Shinjuku—sort of like the red-light district of Tokyo—which was really hard to do, because I spoke almost no Japanese. One club hired me as a sort of pet; I was the only foreigner there. It was really boring because all I did was sit there and smile, holding my little dictionary. This was a big bar with a large dance floor, and they had professional entertainment. Every night was different. They would have a Japanese drumming group in, then transvestites doing a strip number, then a professional rakugo story-teller."

Some of the drawbacks of the nightclub business soon became apparent to Karen. "The customers fed me, which was OK, but it was a long haul home, and since it was late, I had a lot of problems with dirty old men on the train. I got off work about midnight. The other women would stay until one or so." Karen's club had about thirty or forty women working. "A variety of women worked there, not all young girls. There were older, divorced women who were down to earth. They were kind and liked to joke.

"Some of the customers were the curly permed *yakuza* types, men coming in with missing fingers, showing off. The *yakuza* were treated with a lot of awe. I knew who and what they were, but to me they were just customers. I was never asked to work specifically for *yakuza*, never had them recruit me for anything. They were always polite, ignoring me at worst."

Karen had lived on the outskirts of Tokyo, but soon moved into the city. "A man I met at that Shinjuku bar—one of the few men who spoke English—was one of the reasons I left the bar and moved into the city proper. He was youngish and very charming. He had spent a lot of time in the States and liked foreign people. I'm not naive, so I was aware of the fact that being a foreigner and a hostess makes people think that I'm for sale or something. But he asked me to work in his office, and I decided to give it a shot.

"We arranged for him to pay me ¥200,000 a month. I told him that I still wanted to hostess at night, and he said that was fine, but that I ought to move from Shinjuku to Ginza, where hostesses make the most money. So I started working in his office, and the inevitable happened, we started having a relationship. I was very upset when I found out he was married. He hadn't mentioned anything and there were no warning signs. I don't believe in having an affair with a married man, so I broke it off. But I still worked in his office, and he was very kind and helpful; he became a long-term friend.

"He continued to be my customer and even helped me get my first job at a Ginza club, Club Chartres. He negotiated the pay for me. I got ¥18,000 a night for less than four hours. He would come in as my customer, buy his bottle of whiskey and chat with me. He also helped me find an apartment, and subsidized part of it. There was no relationship, though; I was seeing other men. He was just very supportive.

"I even met his wife, though I didn't really want to. She was a wonderful, sexy, intelligent woman who spoke English perfectly. I couldn't figure out why he'd had an affair, though it seems normal for Japanese men. She insisted that we go to Nikko together, a day trip. She told me that she was very upset, that she knew her husband was seeing someone, though she didn't know why or who it was. I could tell from her story that she wasn't referring to me, but I could see that she gradually began to think it was. I could see what was happening, though I couldn't explain it all to her."

Besides learning about the common Japanese wife-mistress scenario, Karen also learned more about the hostessing business. "Working in Ginza was my first experience in a big-money club with big-paying customers. Men easily spent ¥60,000 to ¥100,000 an evening. Of course, the customers pay the most when they first come in, because they have to pay ¥10,000 to ¥30,000 for the initial bottle of whiskey, usually cheap Japanese whiskey that they could buy at a store for ¥2,000 or ¥3,000. At this place, they would pour the whiskey into fancy decanters to look impressive. At other bars, I've seen them pour cheap Suntory Old into Johnnie Walker Red bottles, and tap water into mineral water bottles.

"This club also had an incentive system for the hostesses. There was a list of our names on the back of the door in a minuscule changing room; a hostess would get an hour's worth of wages tacked on if a customer asked for her by name. We could also go out to dinner with a customer, come in an hour late, and get paid for that hour as well as an extra hour's wages when the customer walked through the door. I'd get paid ¥8,000 to go out for dinner, get fed, come in at 9:00 instead of 8:00. But you have to go into something deeper to get customers in like that; most of them don't take you out to dinner just because they like your face. There's a lot of screwing around, love affairs, illegitimate children, jealousy, and back stabbing in this business. Many of the women are sleeping with their customers.

"There was a really brash and pushy Brazilian girl at that bar who insisted on customers taking her out for dinner. They fired her because the customers were feeling pressured. I remember her screaming in the middle of the bar when they fired her. Here's this restrained piano music in the background, and she's yelling, 'You fucking pricks!' I thought, good for her, because they tell you to do something, and then you do it so well that they don't like it. Of course, you need to use a certain amount of tact. She wasn't aware of that, but the Japanese aren't always very tactful, either, even though there's usually a thin veneer of it."

Karen's ex-lover and boss stayed on the scene. "He would sometimes call in sick at the club for me, then pay me the wages I lost. We'd go out for a hoot, go out drinking in Roppongi, or to a transvestite bar. I continued to work at his office for about ten months. I left that bar after about four or five months, because I wasn't pulling my weight by going out with other customers. He was sort of a buffer, because he was a paying customer and they knew if they lost me they'd lose him, too."

Karen moved to a club across the street called Eau d'Amour. "That was my first experience with out-and-out prostitution. The mama was a really sleazy woman, and her customers were really disgusting. Birds of a feather flock together. She obviously slept with her customers; she'd be rubbing their crotches under the table. She was a glorified prostitute who kept her old customers and they all grew old together. They'd get a piece on the side and she'd adjust their bill, and they were happy together. But the Western women there didn't like the level of clientele, and I don't mean just the monetary level, I mean attitude level."

Infighting among the hostesses soon became an issue for Karen at Eau d'Amour. "One of the older women, a hostess who was second-in-command under Mama, had a customer—a very nice older man, really quite a gentleman—who came in almost every night. One night he invited three or four Western girls to go out and have a snack with him. He had a hired car, which a lot of top executives have in Tokyo, and since we were going home in the same direction, he dropped me off at my apartment, a perfect gentleman.

"The next time he came to the bar, the second-in-command hostess wouldn't let me sit at his table. I couldn't figure out why. A couple of nights later she brought in pictures of a baby at a playground. The next time he came in, he actually requested that I sit at his table, and she said no. It clicked with me that the baby was his kid, and that she saw me as some kind of threat, even though I showed no interest in him at all. She'd gotten herself knocked up and he'd be paying the rent for the rest of his life. Because of this incident I was fired. The mama wouldn't listen to me when I told her I had no interest in the man; all that mattered to her was that her longest-standing hostess was unhappy, and she was sorry, but I'd have to leave."

Karen soon saw another side to the business. "I moved to a famous place in Akasaka—Club Kato—and this is where I came into contact with Western prostitution. The mama-san there was the long-term mistress of a man with whom she'd had a child. There was a wide range of customers at Club Kato, many of whom spoke English very well."

Karen noticed that certain customers would come back to see certain girls. "I couldn't understand why a guy would come back for, say, a girl named Laura. She didn't always sit at his table, and she wasn't particularly nice to him. But one night when I left the bar to catch a train I noticed her getting into a taxi with this guy.

"What I didn't know was that the mama was a pimp. The bar would charge the customer ¥60,000 to ¥80,000, pocket ¥20,000, and the girl would get ¥40,000 or ¥60,000. These girls weren't what I would look at and consider prostitute material. But in Japan, I guess just being white and easy is what counts. Some Western women actually have it easier as prostitutes in Japan. Extremely tall blondes are so alien to most Japanese men that some of them claim they almost never have to touch a customer. Many of the men are so overwhelmed that they simply stare in awe and pay without having done anything. There were six white women, four Filipinas, and about six Japanese women working at that bar. The Filipinas were expected to hook. I was never approached to do it.

"One night the topic came up with Laura, and I told her I didn't want to insult her, but if the guys were rat-faced grease balls, how could she do it? Very few of the men were attractive at that club. Obviously money was a factor. She said, 'Honey, you put a condom on them, they shoot in five minutes, and you go home. I don't have to go to a bar and chat them up and smell their bad breath and hope that they take me shopping. It's five minutes with a condom. They come quickly, and they know nothing about foreplay. You don't have to put up with anything else, you just go home.'

"But I still don't see how a woman could be a prostitute," Karen continued. "If a man's attractive, I do it for free. If I want to take him as a lover or if I just want a one-night stand, that's my business. And I'm not going to give my bar ¥20,000. If the guy wants to pay me money, that's fine, although I've never been given any. One guy asked me if I wanted a new dress for work and I said yes. He was a nice man, a family man. There was an air of sexuality, but nothing happened. If a man wants a hooker there are plenty of places to go."

Though the money of prostitution was an attraction for these girls, it didn't seem that they saved much of it. "One girl told me she turned a couple of tricks a week, making anywhere from ¥80,000 to ¥100,000. She said she'd book into some place like the Imperial Hotel and blow the money, just because she felt she deserved it. These girls aren't pros. They are girls who are seduced by the money. They can't deal with the guilt."

Getting and giving respect was another issue for Karen. "I led a double life, teaching English and having this responsible image, and then throwing some makeup and jewelry on and becoming a hostess. I was always afraid that someone from one of my other jobs would come in and see me. During the summer, I used to stop for ice cream on the way to the club. I wouldn't be dressed for work, because with police and immigration officials around, you might get noticed. One day the mama-san started giving me shit about eating in the street— Japanese don't eat outside—and lowering the image of her club. This is a woman who is an obvious sleazy prostitute, giving me a hard time about eating ice cream. I guess a customer had seen me and mentioned it."

Problems with this mama didn't end. "Once a customer tried to grab my breast, and I didn't like that kind of thing, so I took his hand away and said 'Please don't do that.' Then this ratbag mama came over and took his hand and put it on her breast, and said, 'In Japan, it's considered a compliment.' That was her attitude. I could manage to keep men from touching me, but of course we were considered *henna gaijin* [strange foreigners]. One Israeli girl slapped a guy because he put his hand right up her skirt. The guy actually kind of enjoyed it and everybody had a good laugh, luckily for her."

There were women Karen looked up to, though not many. "I can say that there were only a couple of women that I respected in that business. One was Mariko at Club Kato, the second-in-command. She was just so nice, motherly, and charming. She could handle anyone. The Hell's Angels could walk in and she could make them sit up and beg. I wish I could take her and transplant her into a place where she could be appreciated.

"There was one man who came in who thought he was the sexiest thing and that we were all just going to jump on him. He was from some small island, old and ugly with warts and bad teeth. Somebody was wining and dining him over a land deal or something. He did just what shouldn't be done, which is to take seriously all the attention you get from hostesses and get pissed out of your head. You can't enjoy all the wonderful food and attention if you're drunk, making a fool of yourself and embarrassing your host. This guy started knocking over drinks and grabbing women while speaking in some awful dialect. They called Mariko over. She shuffled over in her kimono and said in her sweet voice, 'This isn't Shinjuku, you know.' Finally, she put her arm around him and he fell asleep with his head on her shoulder. She's really good at what she does."

Karen doesn't see the rosy future that others do for the hostessing business. "The men know it's deception, and they've been sucked in long enough. Many times I've thought if only I had the money to open my own bar, we could have backgammon and play classical music. Forget *karaoke*. I don't believe a lot of people like *karaoke*. The majority of men would rather be home with their families. A lot of the younger guys don't like the hostess business, they feel it's really shallow and manipulative, which it is. It's bad whiskey. They would much rather be out with their own ladies. I think the new breed of Japanese coming up are more open minded and believe more in equality, but I think it's going to take another generation for things to really change."

Like Carrie and Debbie, Karen knows that time spent in the *mizu shobai* changes perceptions and attitudes. "After a couple of years, I found myself feeling that I was a professional hostess, or as professional a hostess as a Westerner could be. I viewed it as a sociological study. I was being paid to act. Sometimes the Japanese like sarcasm. They'd ask me what color my pubic hair was, and I'd come back with, 'The same color as my eyes, of course. Your pubic hair is black and your eyes are black, so of course my pubic hair is blue.' And they'd believe it, until I laughed."

Being accepted into the inner circle is an age-old problem for foreigners in Japan, no matter what business they're in. "I got along well with the customers, and when I'd move to another club, the guys would try to go to that club, but the new clubs would never accept them, because the Japanese don't think Westerners understand their mentality. And that's what pissed me off. I did the whole thing with the clothes, which I wouldn't have worn anywhere except the clubs. A lot of girls thought the guys were idiots, twelve-year-olds, for asking what color their pubic hair is, and I'd say, 'No kidding, but what do you think you're getting paid for?' No matter where I went, the Japanese hostesses would move up in the ranks, making bonuses here and bonuses there, and I was working just as hard, but I was never given a bonus or incentive. I was always just another Westerner, even though I could probably surpass many of the Japanese women, without having to sleep with the men. But they never allowed me to play their game. They'd tell me I was too smart, advise me to 'Put some bows in your hair.' They criticized me for forcing sophisticated conversations, not realizing that I wasn't the one bringing up politics and religion. A lot of men were bored, and when they found someone they could talk to, they wanted to. They're not stupid. These are the movers and shakers of Japan. They're well travelled and well educated. When they come in and you treat them like kids, they'll go along with it, but they don't necessarily want it that way."

Karen explained other problems and limitations of being a foreigner in the bar business. "A lot of places would photocopy your visa or passport, even though that's none of their business. Only the sleazy places did that, oddly enough. Australians and New Zealanders can work legally as hostesses with their visas, but it still doesn't look good to work at a bar. I couldn't believe that some of the Australians I knew would list their clubs as their employers.

"I don't like working at places with Australians or Filipinas because the police come in and check them out. I've never been busted, but I've always been very careful. Tourist visas are no good for working at clubs these days. What foreigners don't understand is that at one point they might have been a valuable commodity, but now there's a glut. The clubs can pick and choose. A lot of girls come in accepting really low wages, and that brings it down for everyone."

Visa and pay problems are not the only frustrating issues Karen and other hostesses deal with. "I've heard some crazy things from customers," Karen says. "One guy said to me, 'Oh, your skin is so lovely and white. I'd like to tattoo it and make a lampshade out of it.' I asked him if he'd spent any time in Germany, and he said yes, he had, as a matter of fact. Another guy just wouldn't take no for an answer. 'How much? How much? How much?' I said I wasn't for sale. He got pissed off. Some of the Japanese men are really sick, maladjusted."

Looking beyond the distasteful behavior, Karen started to see why Japanese society is the way it is. "The hostess trade allows these guys to feel like playboys. There's never been a time in their lives when they can date. They get married; they have kids; they might have an affair here or there. But the hostess business is one place that allows them to flirt with women, and it doesn't endanger their marriage. A forty-year-old man acts like an eighteen-year-old kid because when he was eighteen he never dated girls. A lot of the men in their fifties, sixties, and seventies told me that the first words they learned after WW II were, 'I'm hungry. Give me food. Give me chocolate. Do you want to buy a watch? Do you want to buy my sister?' They were poor. They formed these companies and worked from nothing. So they are gods, in a way. They're used to getting their own way, and they can have anyone they want. A girl is just another trophy. But with this power comes a certain attitude toward those who are less powerful. They crawled up from the ashes, and they had no time for kindness or sensitivity. These are men who actually respected foreigners, because they knew what it was like to get their asses kicked. They knew they were wrong in the war. A lot of them were anti-war, but they went and fought. They say they were betrayed by their country. 'We were brainwashed. Now we're beating you economically. It's just another invasion.'

"One guy said to me once, 'We conquered the Philippines and slaughtered the Filipinos. And we're doing it these days, too. We take their women, we rob them of their economic power, and they are our slaves, the same way the Koreans are.' That guy frightened me, but his views are not uncommon in Japan. The Japanese are heavily into S & M. It's a very subtle form of a power play that goes on with men and women. I heard of a place that was just busted in Akasaka, a club where they were giving live enemas on stage." Karen shudders. "Is that erotic? Enemas? What do they do for sex? People pay to see this. You walk down the street and see the posters. There are S & M hotels. What are these people doing? I feel so sorry for their wives."

Karen's view on the bar business is bleak. "Nowadays, forget it—you can't open up your own bar, there's no way. You wouldn't last. These women who are mamas now started in the hostess trade when it was young. They've made a lot of money, and they have no heart left. They're cruel, cold, mean, calculating people. But because of this drive, they are successful. A lot of these women came from some armpit fishing village, woke up and said, 'I've got brains, I've got a body, I'm smart, I'm going to go to Tokyo and make something of myself.' And that's what they did—they clawed their way out. There's no room for nice people in the club business. That's my biggest sorrow. It will be the end of the hostess business. The competition, the manipulation— Japanese men don't want that anymore. Young people don't like it; as all men do, they love to be pampered and babied, but they're not stupid, and they're not children. There must be a level of respect."

Karen has also observed the inner politics of bars. "What holds the whole mishmash together are the 'boy-sans,' the bartenders, the guys who crawl across the floor with the trays in their hands. They are amazing. The knees of their pants are baggy from crawling across the floor to these bastards. The Japanese hostesses just snap their fingers and say, 'Ice!', and the guys come crawling. It's a very funny reversal of the male-female roles, where the women are really strong and the guys are subservient. Never underestimate their power, though. They watch, they know what's going on. If you're a good hostess they'll stick up for you, but you have to be nice to them."

Foreign businessmen are often treated to a night out on the town, which includes entertainment at a hostess bar. "I had two weird experiences in Japan. A guy from Texas came into the bar. He was a real Texan with the big belly, the solid gold belt buckle, and fancy shoes, and he came up and said, 'My name's Tex. You're a pretty little thing. How much, honey?' I played stupid. I wanted to see him squirm. And I said, 'I'm sorry, for what?' He kept pushing with, 'You know what I mean. How much?' I kept playing stupid. He kept pushing me until I had to tell him I wasn't for sale. 'You mean to say you're sitting here next to me drinking my whiskey and getting me all excited and you're not for sale?!' He wouldn't believe me, no matter how much I tried to explain the Japanese system to him. He wouldn't give up.

"But I had my worst experience with some white South Africans. I heard this weird English across the bar and figured out where they were from. I asked the mama not to seat me there, but she sent me anyway. At this bar, we also had this bit where you had to sing a song dressed up in a samurai outfit, with a sword and a cape and a Japanese hair wig, and they'd take photos. One guy said, 'Oh, you look like a wog,' which is of course a derogatory term. I was being really patient with these people. When we had our first drink, I made a toast to Nelson Mandela. They just stopped. Then I added, 'and to Pieter Botha.' I was so disgusted. I don't think South Africans like the Japanese because they aren't white, even though they give them honorary white status. I could even see their attitude toward the Japanese at the table. Then they had the audacity to ask me how much, and I thought I'd rather die."

Karen found herself slipping into the hostess lifestyle. "I like the idea of being paid to drink, but I found myself drinking a lot, smoking a lot, and not going to bed till 4:00, 5:00, or 6:00 in the morning. My boyfriends hated it, because we didn't have any time together. And because they were Japanese, they wanted to be babied, and they were very jealous." Karen stuck with it anyway, and tried to keep her head on straight. "I never gave up my pride. I never sold myself. A lot of guys buy hostesses dresses or jewelry. The girls get confused with the fact that men are buying good service. Japanese men love to spend money on you so you remember their name when they walk in the club. You give them good service and jump up when they come in. They'll pay for that. If you can accept that and not let it go to your head, then you have a place in this business."

Chapter Seven

WOMEN AT A DISCOUNT: *JAPAYUKI-SAN*

The white Western women's perspective on Japan is colored by the fact that, though treated differently from Japanese, they usually fare better than non-white non-Japanese. A trip to a special bar on the outskirts of Kyoto introduces women in Japan's *mizu shobai* who not only get no respect, but who are also often in danger.

As my taxi brings me south of the city, the colored lights and jumbled buildings of downtown Kyoto give way to the dark greenery of winding mountain roads. At 10:00 p.m., we pull into the parking lot of a glowing nightclub that seems to have appeared out of nowhere. The place is packed. Once inside, I note that the club's interior is quite spacious by the standard of most Japanese bars. There's a large video screen, dance floor, and white grand piano.

The place is filled except for one corner table. At each table of men sits at least one woman, just as at any other hostess bar in Japan, but the women aren't Japanese. They're Filipinas. Mama is the exception— an overweight, worn-out-looking Japanese woman stuffed into a tight dress, her face buried in pasty foundation and blood-red lipstick. The mama's haggard appearance is in sharp contrast to the pretty young women around her. But the customers show up here for the girls, not the mama.

At 19, Lena is the club's youngest hostess. At 11:00 p.m., she disappears behind a curtain. The lights go down, the music goes up, and Lena steps out in a silver bikini, spike heels, and a synthetic pink feather boa. The strip show is on. Lena is a good dancer; she practiced at a school in Manila before coming to Japan. In fact, all the women at the school trained for entertainment careers in Japan. Like Lena, they came looking for big money.

The bikini top is off, and Lena holds the boa in just the right position to give viewers the illusion that they're seeing something they aren't. She disappears behind the piano, comes back in the G-string that was under her bikini, and lies backward on the stool she's carried out with her. A few dexterous twists and the pink fluff flows between her extended legs, and Lena's up again, this time with no panties. The lights are dimmed even further, and Lena makes a round of all the tables, smiling at each customer, feather boa flowing in a manner both provocative and self-protective. A dazzling swirl at the last table and she disappears behind the curtain.

"How did you like my show?" Lena asks jokingly after joining our table. She smiles at a compliment on her dancing. "I get paid more than the other girls because I do the nude dance." This is not Lena's first stay in Japan. "I was here working at another place last year. My agency in Manila sends me wherever the Japanese production company wants me. Some girls come here on tourist visas and work illegally, but I have a legal six-month working visa."

Our conversation is in English, so the mama at the next table can't listen in. "I hate the mama," Lena says, scrunching up her nose. "She acts nice while we're working in the club, but she's awful when we're not. She's always trying to cheat us out of our money, too. Mama's husband owns this club. I think he's a *yakuza*." Lena starts talking about the customer at our table, a friend of a friend and my ticket into this club. "He promised me a television before I go back to the Philippines. See this dress? He bought it for me in Osaka." She smiles at the customer and asks how the dress looks, but he doesn't remember that it's the one he bought for her. She puts her hand in his back pocket and grins teasingly when she escorts him upstairs to a taxi. Lena has already learned how to get the most out of her time in Japan.

Lena is one of thousands of young Southeast Asian women who have poured into Japan, especially during the mid to late 1980s, to work in the sex industry. The women are called *japayuki-san*, a term that came into popular use after the publication of a controversial book of the same name by Tetsuo Yamatani in 1985. The term is derived from *karayuki-san*, the name given to the tens of thousands of women who left Japan at the end of the nineteenth century to become prostitutes in Southeast Asia. *Kara* was a reference to China, and *yuki* means "to go." *Karayuki-san* were Japanese women who "went to China," or went far away, while the current *japayuki-san* refers to "those who go to Japan."

Aside from the thousands of women that immigration authorities catch each year working illegally in the *mizu shobai* on tourist visas, there are many more women who manage to get cultural or student visas from Japanese language schools so that they can legally stay longer. Their names conveniently appear in roll books, even though they rarely attend classes. The schools get their tuition, and the "students" get their visas. There has been a crackdown on this kind of activity, but it has not been eliminated. Though there are male manual laborers from countries like Bangladesh and Pakistan using the same tactic to stay in Japan and work, the women far outnumber the men.

These people come to Japan because the money they can make is far greater than what they can earn in their own countries. According to figures from a Japanese television documentary on the problem, women in the Philippines who work as maids make the equivalent of ¥1,800 per month, a schoolteacher makes about ¥10,000 per month, and a go-go dancer-prostitute about ¥20,000 a month. A Filipina in Japan working as a hostess or stripper can pull in at least ¥100,000 a month, even after the "production company" that has recruited the woman takes its ample cut.

A young Japanese woman friend who worked as a dental hygienist once told me something that confirmed the stories I had heard about Southeast Asians trying to make a living pleasing men. "We had a young Thai woman in the other day, and she asked the dentist to pull out all of her front teeth, even though they were perfectly healthy and she had a nice smile. I later asked the dentist why she would want to do something that was obviously a waste and not good for her. He said it was to make her business easier." This young Thai woman was "customizing" her mouth, as many hundreds of others in her business have, to lower the chances of irritating her male customers with teeth scraping against their penises.

A visit to the Philippines made the reasons for women wanting to work in Japan clear to me. At the end of our stay, my travel partner and I had time to kill before catching a plane back to Osaka, and out of curiosity went into one of the many go-go bars on Manila's famed Mabini Street, one of Asia's busiest "meat" markets. As the women danced in their macrame string bikinis, were pawed by the audience (none of whom were Filipino; this is a tourist industry), and went to back rooms with private customers, their faces were devoid of expression. They were doing their job, that's all. Though most of them looked as if they'd been in the business for a while, one woman had such an untarnished, innocent smile that she might have frightened customers away by her apparent lack of vocational know-how. I was in close enough range to have a conversation with her.

She told me she had been working at the bar for all of two weeks, which accounted for her innocent appearance. At twenty-two, she had already quit working at a bank because the money at the go-go bar was better. A customer would pay forty pesos (¥2,000 at the time) for spending time with her, and of that, she would get to keep sixteen pesos (¥800, not quite six U.S. dollars). The bar takes the rest.

It's easy to see why Philippine women search for work abroad. Almost anyplace would give them a better opportunity to make a living and send money home to support their families than their own country. Singapore and Hong Kong are overflowing with Filipina maids, women who are too old to make it in the entertainment business, or who are young enough, but who don't want to compromise themselves. The assassination of Benigno Aquino made 1983 a boom year for Philippine people searching for work abroad. In 1982, the *japayuki* population was dominated by Taiwanese women, but Filipinas were in the lead by 1983. The number of Korean and Taiwanese *japayuki-san* continue to drop as both countries' economies get stronger. Women from Thailand and other Southeast Asian countries make up another significant portion of the japayuki-san population, as do women from Colombia.

Japayuki-san started presenting major problems to Japanese immigration officials in the mid 1980s. The gangster-run production companies that go directly to Bangkok or Manila to recruit women are a main factor in the *japayuki* problem, but it's hard to infiltrate the production companies without extended questioning of the women who have turned themselves in or been caught in club raids. Immigration simply doesn't have the facilities to keep so many women long enough to question them about their bosses and connections in Japan. For the police, women being locked up and forced into prostitution is less of an issue than the growing narcotics problem.

The explosion of a hand grenade on Thai Airways' flight 620 from Bangkok on October 16, 1986, stirred up trouble for Thai Airways as well as for Japanese immigration and customs officials. The incident exposed the ease with which weapons were being smuggled into Japan from Bangkok and Manila. Christened the "*japayuki* flight" by the newspapers, flight 620 had become a veritable shuttle service for women coming to Japan to start their club careers, many of whom became unwitting smugglers. Suitcases packed with guns and drugs have often been carried in by girls who had no idea what they were carrying. Reporters at the airport photographed men trying to match photos with women who had just stepped off the plane. Some women wore special colors or other identifying marks for their escorts. Once outside the gates, the men drove their wards off to a new life in one of Japan's flashy entertainment districts.

The problem got so out of hand in the late 1980s that both police and immigration officials started a serious crackdown. Things got tougher at clubs and bars, airports and language schools. But as soon as one tactic for entering Japan is curbed by the authorities, another one pops up. As the government imposes stricter regulations and requires more papers from entering aliens, forgery services increase. The walls of Japanese consulates in cities like Manila and Bangkok are plastered with names and photos of illegal aliens. Even the cosmetics and coiffure industries have prospered as a result of the demand for hairstyle and face changes by women who wish to avoid being recognized by immigration officials on the lookout for second and third time offenders.

For the thousands of illegal aliens floating around Japan without passports or with forged papers, the lack of official identification can be both boon and bane. Forged papers may prevent immigration officials from booting illegal *japayuki-san* out of the country; but according to a *yakuza* on the inside, forged papers or no identification at all make the women unidentifiable, and thus easily disposable. A young girl with no proper identification who is found by gangster bosses to be too much of a problem may end up floating face down in one of Japan's many polluted rivers, never to be identified. Not only will the police spend little time on investigating the death of an unidentifiable Filipina hostess, but sometimes temptation is too hard to resist, even for those who are supposed to protect victims. In the late 1980s, one newspaper carried the story of an Osaka policeman who had four Filipinas locked in his apartment. He was selling them as prostitutes.

In the words of one of the many *japayuki-san* "brokers" and production company bosses working in Manila and Osaka, "This is a business, and in this business those girls are merchandise. If we thought of them as human beings, there's no way we could run these operations. They are items to sell and trade, and we get as much as possible out of them while we have them."

Not everyone involved in the *japayuki-san* business is quite as cold-hearted, and not everyone is a *yakuza*. "I'm not involved in selling women," says a respectable marriage broker. "I just arrange false marriage certificates. Sure, I get some money out of it, but I really feel I'm in it to help people. I get calls from women who want to stay in Japan and work for a few years, and they need a permanent visa to do that legally. I get them set up in a marriage on paper so they can stay and work. It makes me happy to be able to help people in trouble."

The marriage racket doesn't always work so ideally, though. Mail-order bride schemes are gaining in popularity as, with young people flocking to the cities, Japanese farmers face a frustrating lack of prospective wives. Korean, Philippine, and Thai women come to Japan to marry in response to ads placed in local papers, and some of these marriages work out. If the woman can adjust to Japan's notoriously xenophobic customs and prejudices, she may actually live a decent life. Some men, however, use the bartered bride technique to acquire women as extra sources of income, forcing their "wives" to work as hostesses and prostitutes. Corazon Aquino's Philippine government cracked down on mail-order bride advertisements under pressure from citizens who want to protect their young women. Nonetheless, thousands of Filipinas come to Japan of their own accord.

The era of the strong yen has made Japan a dreamland for people not just from third-world countries, but also from Europe and North

America. Japan wasn't always the economic superstar it is today, and *japayuki-san* didn't always flood the Japanese club world. In fact, the situation was the reverse in the not too distant past. At the end of the nineteenth century, Japan was sending tens of thousands of *karayuki-san* to sell their bodily wares in such faraway places as Africa, Australia, Siberia, Manchuria, and yes, even to Bangkok, Manila, and Singapore.

Amakusa in Kyushu's Kumamoto prefecture was the heart of the *karayuki* business. Not all Japanese women who went abroad as prostitutes were from Amakusa, but the majority were, partly because of the overwhelming poverty in the area. The shame of this association with prostitutes affected local politics and education; schools have done their best to keep the *karayuki-san* issue out of the history books. Not only did the money the *karayuki-san* made help support families back in poor fishing villages, but one man who made his fortune smuggling these women abroad went so far as to say, "Selling women is for the good of our country!"

Economics may be the key factor in the *karayuki-san* phenomenon, but not everyone's story is that simple. Some women were just out for freedom and adventure. One of the few living *karayuki-san* willing to speak about her early life working overseas said that she didn't want to spend her whole life trapped in a country town. Going abroad to work was a fad at the time, so this woman went with her husband to Malaysia to work on a rubber plantation. He suddenly died when she was twenty-nine, and she ended up being a prostitute to support herself. While other women at the time went abroad knowing they would be prostitutes, there were also many like this woman who ended up in that position through unexpected hardship.

NINA, LUISA, AND FLOR

The *japayuki-san* of today have their own reasons for coming to Japan. The overriding factor for most is a need for money, primarily to support a hungry family back home. There is also a sense of leaving their own country on a lark, for a taste of freedom. With the strict Catholic upbringing many Filipinas have, it is a pleasure just to get away and try something different. Three friends, all from Manila, discuss their experiences working in bars in Japan. Nina, twenty-four and the eldest, speaks with confidence. Luisa, twenty, looks like a country tomboy, not typical club material. Flor, nineteen and very pretty, has the most to say about working in Japan's clubs, because she is on her second six-month stint as a bar hostess.

Nina tells why she came to Japan. "I graduated from college in the Philippines with a Bachelor of Science in Business Administration, majoring in marketing. After graduation I applied for a job. Every day I'd buy the newspaper and start calling places. I'd go to offices. I'd start at 8:00 in the morning and keep going until 5:00. I covered the whole town. I'd ask the security guards if there were any vacant positions in the building, and they'd say no. I tried for two or three months to get a job, but unfortunately there weren't any.

"I'd heard about work in Japan, but mostly I'd heard bad things. I didn't know what really happens here. All the Filipinas who went to work in Japan came back with electronic equipment like stereos or TVs, and they had a lot of money. In the Philippines, especially in the place we're from, if you have so many things, people think you must have done something bad." This is Nina's subtle way of saying that the girls who came back with all this wealth were assumed to have been prostitutes.

"Some Filipinas come to Japan by connection with Japanese men who go to Manila and recruit them. We came through an agency. After applying to the agency, we had to practice singing and dancing for about three months, but we didn't have to pay for lessons." Who ran the agency, Japanese gangsters or Filipinos? "First we met Philippine people at the agency, and later we met Japanese people. They were waiting for us when we came to Japan. One of the guys signed our papers when we arrived. We already had a visa arranged before we left home." Did this make entering the country easy? "The immigration officials let us in, but they were unfriendly to us. I don't think they like people from the Philippines."

Boyish Luisa adds, "My parents weren't happy about my coming to Japan, but it's my own decision." Does she like Japan enough to want to come back? "I don't like many things about being in Japan, but I'll come back again if I can because of the freedom."

Flor explains, "That's it in one word—freedom. We can get together with other Filipinas, do whatever we want, and go home whenever we want. In the Philippines, our parents don't let us smoke and drink, they think we're too young to do that."

They sound like rebellious teenagers in some ways, but they are fairly adult about saving their money. Luisa puts her money in the bank, some in the Philippines, some in Japan. "I have three brothers and one sister. I'm the youngest, so I don't really have to support them."

As the eldest of five children, Nina is responsible for her family's welfare. "I have to work to support them. They expect me to send money to them, but my mother doesn't force me to send a certain amount every month."

Flor's motives are not based on family needs, since she's an only child, and she has ambiguous feelings about her host country. "This is my second time in Japan. When I went back to the Philippines after my first stay, I said I would never come back to Japan because I had many bad experiences, but three months ago, I changed my mind. I don't know why. Then I told my friends to come with me. They're here for the first time. We like it sometimes, but we have mixed feelings."

Nina continues, "We have some Japanese friends here, but not real friends. A hostess might smile and treat you well when she introduces the customers, but she just does it for the sake of the job. Sometimes if a hostess comes to the club with a guy who's her boyfriend, she doesn't like us talking with him. If we do, she gets jealous. She can't show us directly that she's jealous, but we can feel it."

Flor describes unpleasant situations that reveal prejudice against her and her friends. "The mama and the manager of my club are good to me, but the hostesses aren't so nice. Sometimes I don't feel good and don't want to drink much whiskey, and one of the hostesses makes my drink really strong. Then I might say something to a customer about not being able to drink much, and the hostess gets really angry at me and says something bad about me to the customer. . . . And did you hear the news story about a Filipina with AIDS? I think they are trying to say bad things about us. Of course we feel hurt. Japanese people treat Americans and Filipinos like they're stupid. They're selfish. They want their country to be number one."

Despite the feelings of rejection and suspicion these three friends have felt from some Japanese people, they all consider themselves lucky not to have met the same fate that many *japayuki-san* do—being locked up in an apartment without their passports. Nina, Luisa, and Flor live in relative freedom, unlike many young Filipinas working in Japan. Luisa was lucky enough to have connections before she came to Japan, making her living situation better than most. "I have an aunt who lives here. She married a Japanese man. I asked the production company for permission to live separately from the other girls, and they said OK, so Nina and I live together with my aunt and her husband."

Still, Luisa can't help but compare the Japanese and Filipino sense of hospitality. "Even though it's my aunt's house, we each pay ¥31,000 a month: ¥25,000 for rent and the rest for utilities. We get to use a bedroom, the kitchen, and the bathroom. That's not the way it would be in the Philippines or America. In Japan, if you stay, you must pay, if you eat, you must buy the food, and we have to cook everything. They don't treat relatives the way they would be treated in the Philippines. Sometimes I'm lonely."

Are their living expenses counterbalanced by the supposedly high pay of the Japanese nightclub world? Nina and Luisa work at the same club, and according to Luisa, "The production company pays us $600 U.S. dollars a month. We get our money from them, not from the club itself."

Flor lives in her own apartment, "the same apartment that I lived in when I was in Kyoto before. Many girls have to go to a different place in Japan every time they come over, but I told my production company that I like Kyoto, and that's the only place I'd go. I pay ¥60,000 a month for my place." She works at a different club from her friends. After paying off her Japanese boss, she finds that there isn't much left to live on, so she moonlights into the wee hours. "After I finish working at the first club, I work at a snack from 1:30 a.m. to sometimes as late as 5:00 a.m. I get ¥1,800 per hour there. I can't save much money, but it's better than the Philippines. I get paid directly by my club, but I have to give half of it to my production company boss. The mama of my club doesn't know that, though. If I told her she'd be mad at them. She's nice."

Handling living expenses isn't the worst of their problems. It makes Luisa angry that "the customers all think that Filipinas need money, so they think we're all prostitutes." Nina adds, "In my case, I just ignore them when they're rude like that. I just smile at them and say nothing."

There have been many adjustments to make, and for Flor, it has meant becoming emotionally tough. "Sometimes the customers tell me that they like me. They say how young and pretty I am. Then the other hostesses get jealous and say bad things about me. Then there are the times when customers grab you in the chest and the crotch, or they hit you. Some of them say, 'Go back to the Philippines. I'll give you the money. You go back right now.' At the first club I ever worked at, I couldn't figure it out. The mama kept telling me that she didn't like Filipinas, but she knew she could get more customers by having me there."

The feeling of prejudice is hard to escape, Luisa points out. "You can tell that people are looking down at you or don't like you by the look in their eyes, even if they talk with you. Some customers won't even talk with you." Not all of the customers are bad, but the nice ones seem few and far between. "Sometimes when we go home, even the taxi drivers get angry for some reason. They ask us if we make a lot of money."

Even with other non-Japanese club workers, Flor has seen problems. "My snack mama is Korean. She doesn't like Filipinas if they don't drink. She only likes Filipinas because they bring customers in. My friend worked at a place from 8:00 p.m. to 2:00 a.m., but she often had to entertain customers until 4:00 a.m. She got no extra money for that, but if she was late at all, she had to pay a penalty fee."

Unfair situations like this, among other things, keep many Filipinas from feeling motivated in their work. "We just want to work and earn money; we don't care how many customers come in," says Nina. "We're always waiting for it to be time to go home. We don't get paid much—

about ¥9,000 a night—so we don't feel that we have to work so hard. We have to give half our earnings to the production agency. If we don't, they will come after us. They have all of our records. We get paid by the club on the last day of each month, and then we go to the agency office in Yamashina and pay them in cash on the first. They convert it to dollars."

Though she gets paid more because she's been here longer and can speak Japanese, Flor still has to pay a large portion to the production agency. "I make ¥11,000 a night at my main club. The agency takes our pay receipts so they know how much we make. We have to give them a percent of our pay, and they also get money from the clubs, more than we get paid. I even have to give the production company half my salary from my side job later at night." Flor has to be careful. She knows about the influence of Japanese gangsters in the business she's in. "The guy at the production office doesn't look like most *yakuza*, but I know he's a *yakuza* boss."

Not everyone is unkind to the girls, but some "friends" may be looking to take advantage of more than what even a second-timer like Flor expects. "I have some friends other than Filipinas. I have one nice Japanese man friend who treats me like a daughter. Sometimes he buys me a dress or a gold pin. He was a customer; the mama is friends with him." Flor tries to make it sound like a perfectly wonderful, innocent friendship, but her tone changes to confusion as she goes on. "He buys me many nice things, but I don't know what he's really thinking. Sometimes I think he wants something else, though he's never tried to get me to go to bed with him. I've never met his wife. Sometimes I think he's afraid she'll find out that he takes me out and buys me things. He has said things about separating from his wife, but I don't like it when he says those things."

Making real Japanese friends may be a challenge for all of these young women, but this is the least worry of many *japayuki-san*. As Nina says, "We are free and not forced to do anything, but many girls are. I have a friend who had to work sleeping with men. For every ¥30,000 she earned, the *yakuza* gave her only ¥10,000. If she wants to go shopping, she has bodyguards. They watch her so she can't move around freely. She didn't like it, so she went back to the Philippines."

Flor has had close experiences with these problems. "My cousin had a bad experience here. She worked like that [sleeping with men] under the *yakuza*. I met her once here in Kyoto at a disco. I asked her how she got here, who brought her from the Philippines. She said the *yakuza* brought her over, and that she had to work at a Turkish bath in Osaka. They kept her passport so she couldn't get away. I have my own passport and a legal visa, so I'm in a better position than she was."

Visas can be a serious issue, as Nina notes. "If you get caught without a proper visa, you have to pay your own way back. If you don't have the money, the Japanese immigration officers send you to Yokohama and make you work until you earn enough to pay for your ticket back."

The experience Flor's cousin had is similar to that of thousands of others. "My cousin didn't know what kind of job it would be when she came over. She came here to make money to support her baby in the Philippines, but it was a mistake. The *yakuza* told her it would be a nice job, just singing and entertaining the customers. Then she got stuck with that bad kind of work and she was always crying. She begged the customers to help her, to tell the police so she could go back to the Philippines, but the customers were afraid of the *yakuza*.

"It's hard to go to the police. When I first came here, I had a friend who was half Filipina and half English, and she's pretty wild. One night we were at a disco and she drank too much. There was also a *yakuza* girl nearby who was drinking too much. Somehow the two of them started arguing. First they were just yelling at each other, but then they started hitting each other. I wanted to call a policeman to come help, but I couldn't speak much Japanese then, and my English isn't very good either, so I felt helpless. Even if I could speak well, they might treat the Japanese girl better. The police don't like foreigners here, especially people from the Philippines."

Overall, despite the sacrifices, the friends still think it was a good idea to come to Japan. They have a life outside of their club jobs. "On our day off, Sunday," says Luisa, "we go to mass at the Catholic church. We like to go out to eat, go to the disco, see the sights. Our salary is not so good, so we don't get to shop very much."

Meeting club expectations takes money, but even in Japan, Flor says they don't make enough money to keep up. "We are lucky to buy one dress in a month. It's hard, because the hostesses look down at you if you wear clothes they don't like. We brought clothes from the Philippines, but we don't have that many. It's hard now, because we don't have warm winter clothes. In the Philippines, many women don't wear stockings, and the club people get angry if you go in without stockings. It's not easy for us to do everything they want."

SEX TOURS

Flor, Nina, and Luisa have all survived their stays in Japan better than many *japayuki-san* do. They are three of thousands who fly to Japan every year to work. But Asian girls don't always have to leave home to earn a living entertaining Japanese men. The multimillion-dollar "Sex Tours in Asia" business boom of the seventies started bringing Japanese customers to them. Even the most respectable of Japan's travel agencies and airlines brazenly advertised group tours inviting men to "enjoy the pleasures of the night" in Bangkok, Seoul, Taipei, Manila, Singapore, and Hong Kong. These tours are still popular, though they have lost steam since the influx of *japayuki-san* and the fear of AIDS. More than one family has been infected by AIDS as a result of a thrill-seeking husband's antics on a group sex tour.

A four-day trip might include daytime bus tours of local sights, but customers reserve their energy and money for the evening's entertainment. Air fare, accommodations, and meals are included in the tour price, but paying for a fresh young bed partner is up to the individual traveler. At sunset in Manila or Bangkok, you might see busloads of Japanese men being wheeled off to their prearranged mass love-trysts. Once at a hotel specially geared for this kind of activity, the tourists are ushered into a room filled with as many as two hundred bikini-clad women marked with numbered badges. In market fashion, each man selects a number, informs his tour manager, pays his fee, and goes to his room to await the arrival of his choice. Lack of manners and style has earned Japanese men a poor reputation among the women who offer them pleasures. The inside nickname for Japanese customers in the Philippines is "monkey banana," referring to tiny, finger-sized bananas—not a reassuring comment for Japanese men, who already suffer from a "small penis complex" (a favorite topic at Japanese bars). But despite their poor manners, the Japanese men remain popular as paying customers along with their top competition, West Germans and Americans.

One Japanese man who has been to these countries says he prefers to go alone rather than on a tour. "I feel stupid being herded around like cattle. I go to the bars where the girls hang out before they go to work. It's more interesting that way." This man has a more adventurous spirit than the average Japanese man. Working for himself, he also has more extended vacations than the average salaryman, who might only have three days for his whirlwind sex tour. "I stayed in the Philippines for quite a while once, when I was younger. I became friends with a pretty young girl from a country area, and I treated her with respect. She brought me to her house to meet her family and they treated me like a king. They fed me and kept giving me a lot to drink. When they got me really drunk, they sent me off with their daughter to a separate shack down the road. Of course I wanted to sleep with her, but I also still had my head about me enough to know that they'd try to make me feel obligated to marry her later. I didn't do it."

He was more than happy to enjoy the pleasures to be had when they were offered for money, however. "I tried to get away from the cities as much as I could. In one area I stayed, there was a place to eat and drink, and you could go to a back room with a girl if you wanted. I figured I would, but it was a really ramshackle place. The girl led me out to a shed with no roof, with a makeshift bed in it. It was like being outdoors. When I started to take my clothes off, I realized that all the guys from the front room were now up on the edges of the walls, leaning in and looking at us. I figured they were just curious, that they wanted to see how a Japanese guy does it, so I went ahead and did it anyway."

Complaints from these Southeast Asian countries, from local municipal officials and women's groups, and protests to the Japanese government itself did little to stop these tours. The more the Japanese came, the more business flourished. A Bangkok newspaper once re-ported that 300,000 women in that city were prostitutes. Still, only a tiny fraction of the profits made on the tours actually fell into local hands. Most of the money went to Japanese airlines, Japanese tour organizers, Japanese hotels, and Japanese-owned restaurants and nightclubs. Real change came only with political and economic changes in the target countries themselves. With increasing friendliness between Japan and Beijing, Japanese tours to Taiwan decreased. Korea's quickly strength-ening economy reduced the necessity for engaging in the skin trade. The assassination of Benigno Aquino and the resulting turbulence in the Philippines made Japanese tourists stay away. Still in dire economic straits, the Filipinas and Taiwanese country girls figured that if Japan wouldn't come to them, they would go to it.

Many of the women who entertained for these tours became the early *japayuki-san*. They were the first to undergo the mass auditions where Japanese *yakuza* "talent scouts" looked over hundreds of young bikini-clad girls, all lining up to smile and parrot what little Japanese they could. After a check for pregnancy stretch marks and a search for that fresh, innocent country look, the lucky ones were told they could go to Japan. Tutored in advance how to answer questions at the airports of Tokyo, Nagoya, and Osaka, even those without long-term visas made it through. Many on fifteen-day visas came in and went into hiding.

Many Japanese are quick to forget their own history of shipping their women out as prostitutes to fight overwhelming poverty, and have little sympathy for the foreign visitors on their soil. From the late 1980s, immigration officials started receiving harsh letters from Japanese women, urging them to get rid of these "dirty, smelly *japayuki-san*." The female residents of one town even went so far as to boycott the local pool when *japayuki-san* women started swimming there. Customers spit in the faces of Filipina hostesses, and no one intervenes. The first Filipina found to have AIDS was quickly deported, and others are pointed at and avoided in public places as potential disease carriers.

Liberal-minded Japanese feel that both male and female migrant workers should be allowed to work legally in Japan to accommodate the need for entertainers and manual laborers. But Japan still resists embracing its poorer neighbors as an economic fact of life and the *japayuki-san* problem is not on the high end of Japan's priorities. However, the trend for Japanese immigration in the 1990s seems to be even stricter about letting foreigners into the country, no matter where they come from. The more obstacles placed in the path of those who want something badly, the more ways they will find to accomplish their goals. As long as Japan has a powerful economy and an entertainment business, there will be hostesses and entertainers from abroad crossing over to its shores. Japan's odd mixture of xenophobia and fascination with foreigners has made a sometimes tragic but important addition to its *mizu shobai* culture.

Chapter Eight

THE GANGSTER ELEMENT

Fingers cut off and presented to the boss for penitence, bodies covered in intricate tattoos, sexual slavery, and killing rival gang members—these are phenomena that the Japanese associate with the country's notorious, Mafia-like *yakuza*. Glorified in films, *yakuza* are more often hated and feared in reality. Ken Takakura, an actor who has appeared in dozens of gangster movies, represents the idolized version of the *yakuza*. He plays one of the vintage gangsters who stood for *giri* and *ninjoo*, a sense of honor, duty, and sympathy for one's fellow man. Unfortunately, this type of Japanese gang member is close to extinction today. The *yakuza*'s power and numbers grow, but when compared to the movies, the quality of their "work" is suffering.

YAKUZA ENCOUNTER

While working at Club Hitomi I had my first glimpse of what these legendary figures were all about. One night, after a call of Lisa, *onegaishimasu!*, I found myself at a table of customers I'd never met before. While bowing my introduction, I had a chance to look the men over. There was something different about them, an aura and appearance that set them apart from other customers. For one thing, they weren't wearing the standard businessman's uniform of a navy-blue or plain-gray suit, but there was something different about their manners, too. While they seemed to be enjoying making small talk with Hitomi's mama, it was not with the wholehearted excitement of the other customers. They were somewhat aloof, as if *they* were in control of the situation, rather than the usual case in the bar of the customer being subtly controlled.

I moved to take my seat. There was something of the usual reaction at seeing Club Hitomi's newly acquired, one and only foreign hostess. *Ahh, beppin-san ya naa!*, they cried, local dialect for, "Oh, what a cute girl!" As far as I could tell, I was in for the typical treatment. Lighthearted flirtation and playful hand holding kept us all busy for a few minutes. Despite the silly nature of the interaction, I sensed that these were not average guys out for some kicks. They certainly didn't act like businessmen on a company expense account; it was as if they were playing a game with us.

The man on my left, who looked to be in his mid-thirties, had a moustache and permed hair, was rather slim, wore a casual, all-white pants and shirt outfit, and was adorned with gold chains at the wrist and neck. The man on my right had a much more unique and disturbing appearance. His most distinguishing feature was his right eye, which looked as if it had been gouged out by a cat. In fact, more than anything else, he resembled a cartoon tomcat blown up to life size. Like the creature he resembled, he appeared to have spent a major portion of his life hanging around and fighting in back alleys.

The tomcat man was heavyset, and had a salt-and-pepper crew cut. He wore a dark shirt with a light speckled tie, under an off-white suit that had a gleamy sheen to it. The entire suit seemed to be shifting and changing with its pattern of what looked distinctly like spermatozoa swimming in varying directions. After a few drinks, the conversation turned to his eye-catching suit. "Hey, your suit reminds me of—" "Yeah, I know. That's why I bought it." There were a few more junior-high-school-level comments of the sort that Japanese bar customers seem to thrive on, but again, it was almost as if these men were just playing along, as if they were expected to act this way.

In fact, these customers turned out to be much more enjoyable company than most of the men that came into the club, for the most part because they didn't have the usual "foreigner complex" that most Japanese have. They asked me intelligent questions about where I was from in the States; one of them had traveled quite extensively there himself. Because these people had been exposed to the world more than the average Japanese, who operate to a large degree as if Japan was still a closed country, our conversation was one of the more sophisticated of my hostessing career. The talk continued until the door flung open and another permed young man came in, looking serious. He, too, was dressed in white with gold at his wrist, but his youth made it obvious that he was of lower rank than the others. He was ushered to our table by the manager.

The mood of my two guests changed radically from relaxed and pleasant to concerned and serious when the young man spewed out a few cryptic words. The thin man put down his glass while the fat man quickly finished the last of his drink. With pleasant smiles and thank yous to Mama, they quickly got up and within an instant had disappeared. Mama and one or two hostesses always accompany exiting customers to the bottom floor of the building, hail a taxi, and wave goodbye as they drive away. This time we didn't even take them down in the elevator.

I wondered what could have called the men out so suddenly. It occurred to me that their appearance and actions made them seem suspiciously like the gangsters I'd heard so much about in Japan. After putting two and two together, I decided I'd be better off not asking why they left that way.

While I had enjoyed the company of these men, there were times during our conversation when I sensed that my participation wasn't welcome. One of the charming things about Hitomi's mama was that she didn't claim to be a suave woman of the world, as many mamas do. Not only was this unsophisticated charm a unique way to attract customers away from the slightly business-hardened type of mama, it was also her genuine character. I liked her and enjoyed working the same tables with her, as well as talking with her alone. But her unsophisticated, innocent charm could also carry with it some dangerous side effects.

One evening, the same man in white suit and gold chains came in with an older man I hadn't seen before and a young guy who looked as if he'd just joined the ranks. They sat at the table closest to the door and seemed in no mood for fun and games. Mama had already said a few words of greeting and was sitting next to them when I arrived. I mixed drinks for them and sat down to entertain. But this didn't seem like business as usual. I understood that this was not a social visit but a heavy powwow that totally excluded me and Mama.

The round of drinks I'd mixed sat almost untouched, and when I moved to freshen them, the man in white told me not to bother. The older man was picking on the young guy for not drinking whiskey; Coke was not a manly drink, he said. The man in white warned him to leave the young guy alone and reassured the youth that there was no problem. For what I thought was a group of friends, there seemed to be a lot of friction.

It occurred to me that I was probably called over to their table because I was not a native speaker of Japanese, and less likely to tune into their discussion than the Japanese hostesses. When words like "killed" and "fight" came up, I knew it was wiser to show no signs of recognition. Mama was called away, so I was the only hostess at the table, but they wanted little attention. Though I made a point of keeping my eyes fixed on the table, I couldn't resist the temptation to pick up what it was these Japanese gangsters were saying to each other. When I heard, "But there are a lot of police in that area," followed by another voice answering with amused, hardened sarcasm, "We have a lot of friends among the police," I was tempted to raise my eyebrows in surprise, but I kept a stone face.

I noticed that though I was doing my best to avoid signs of hearing the men's conversation, Mama, who had returned to sit with us, was leaning forward in her seat to hear better, making faces of surprise and fascination as if she were included in their discussion. This was an instance in which her innocent charm was manifesting itself in an unhealthy way, it seemed to me. I didn't want to draw attention to Mama's eagerly listening face, so I looked back down at the table. Once again, it was as if a silent warning had gone off and our guests were suddenly on their feet to go. I decided then that they weren't customers to become too chummy with.

Conversation With A *Yakuza*

The secrets of the mysterious *yakuza* in Japan have been largely uncovered. The history and current trends in the realm of Japan's gangsters, who have infiltrated beyond Asia's borders into our own backyard, is covered in enthralling—and often disturbing—detail in *Yakuza*, a dynamic book by David Kaplan and Alec Dubro. For a broad look at Japan's underworld, this is a useful source of information.

The last thing I ever thought I'd consider a lucky break was unknowingly walking into the home of an influential gangster. I'd been trying to get an interview with a *yakuza* for months, but the actual meeting itself happened by accident. Just days before I left Japan to return to the U.S., I had an in-depth interview with a gangster whose words offer not only an inside view of the *yakuza*'s involvement in Japan's entertainment world, but also a distinct philosophical view of the world.

In an attempt to get one more set of interviews with *mizu shobai* workers, I spent one of my final days in Kyoto going out to meet every last connection I had. One of the women from my office had given me an introduction to her aunt, a former club mama who invited me to come speak with her at her home. I called her from a train station in northern Kyoto, and was told someone would come to pick me up.

An old woman in traditional clothing shuffled down to the station to find me. I was easily identifiable since I was the only foreigner to be seen. She led me silently along narrow footpaths that wove between houses, past rice and vegetable fields, and up to what appeared to me to be a small palace. Houses in Japan are infamous for being tiny and cramped for space, but the building we were approaching was anything but; in fact, it dominated the whole group of houses in the little neighborhood that sat at the foot of one of Kyoto's small, ancient mountains. It was as if this was somehow the guardian villa, the lord's castle that stood above all else in its shadow. I went into the house, and was greeted very pleasantly by my friend's aunt, an attractive woman whose hair was pulled back in the traditional manner appropriate for kimono.

She looked quite young to have been the mama of her own club, though there were cases of very young club proprietresses. It was only much later in our conversation that I was shocked to learn that this lovely woman was well into her fifties, and had been out of the business for years. It was for this same reason that I thought she was the daughter, and not the wife, of the man to whom I was about to be introduced. Before leading me to the room in which the man sat, she quietly and politely mentioned that her niece had told her that I was interested in interviewing a *yakuza*. And though she would be happy to tell me about her years as a club mama, she thought I might like to take the opportunity to interview the man behind the door, a retired *yakuza* himself.

At long last I had a chance to ask questions about the *yakuza* role in the Japanese sex and entertainment business! But how, I thought as I walked through the door and bowed to this man, does one tactfully say, "I want to know about your life as a member of the underworld, a gangster, an outlaw"? Mr. S. (who asked that his identity not be revealed) made things easier by asking me what I wanted to know. The Japanese language offers numerous ways to soften a direct request with layers of politeness, and it was in this way that I told him I wanted to hear about the *yakuza*'s involvement in the *mizu shobai*. Were they as heavily involved as many people believed?

Mr. S. sat in silence, looking at me just long enough to make me uncomfortable. If conducting this interview was going to be this difficult, I figured I'd be better off quitting now. But Mr. S. did not fail me;

he answered all that I asked and more. The only things he didn't talk about specifically were the explicit details of his own life as a gangster. His youthful wife glided across the floor to serve me steaming green tea, and sat attentively next to her aging husband, adjusting the sweater around his shoulders when he looked cold, and adding comments to his tale as he spoke.

"How are the *yakuza* related to the *mizu shobai*?" He repeated my question as if to make sure he'd heard correctly. "Most of the high-class bars in Tokyo are affiliated with *yakuza* in some way or another. One way is as protection. It's like hiring a guard. If you have trouble with anyone who comes into the club, the local *yakuza* takes care of him. You know, just like the big bouncers you see in American movies. It's the same thing.

"The guys don't hang around the club all the time, of course. They come only when called. A club pays an annual fee to a gang, and the gang takes care of any trouble that might come up. Usually the word gets around to other *yakuza* that Club A has a connection with Gang X. If you get a class-A *yakuza* in there, the grade B and C *yakuza* won't come around. They're afraid. What counts is that other *yakuza* know the club is protected. It's just like the territorial system in Al Capone's Chicago. If regular customers knew there was a *yakuza* connection, they might be afraid to come to the club. . . . Do you know about *sookaiya*? They're gangsters that go into company stock meetings to assert influence upon request of certain corporate officials. They save these officials some headaches. It's the same kind of protection. But everyday people can't know about this, or they'd be scared.

"There are thousands of clubs and bars in Kyoto's Gion. I haven't been active there for a few years, so I don't know the exact figures today, but at that time over half the shops in Gion had a *yakuza* connection. There are real advantages to having *yakuza* there. Most important of all is the *yakuza*'s ability to pull good hostesses to a club. It works just like big corporations that have headhunters out trying to find the best executives. A club needs good women to get customers in, and *yakuza* act as headhunters. They make trades, money for women. There are guys whose entire job is going out to entice girls to move from one club to another. If someone tries to pull a girl from a *yakuza*-connected club, however, there's trouble. You don't step into *yakuza* territory and try to pull away their assets without getting a warning.

"How do you get a girl to change clubs? At most clubs there's a sales quota the girl has to meet. It can be the number of customers she brings to the club per month or more directly, a certain amount of profit that she's responsible for. Most customers don't pay directly each time they visit. They're billed or they pay every few visits. If a man doesn't pay his bill, the hostess he is affiliated with is held responsible. If some guy owes a million yen and won't pay, she has to pay it. This is how prostitutes are born. They have to get that money somehow, and fast. That's not the only reason, of course. Guys who come into these bars are paying ¥10,000 for ¥1,000 worth of drinks, so they're looking for something to make up the value. You know how it is with men and their primal instincts. To keep a customer coming to the club, for every hundred times he's there flirting with a hostess, she may have to give out to the guy once, just to keep him hooked.

"At the end of the month, a girl that hasn't been meeting her quota starts to feel the pressure from the club management. That's when one of these 'headhunters' comes along. It's someone she's already talked to, who knows her situation. At the right psychological point, he comes up with an offer. 'Well, I know you're here at Club B, but if you come

over to Club A, they'll pay you ¥700,000 a month instead of ¥500,000.'
Here's a girl who brought in ¥1,000,000 worth of business for her club,
but men still owe ¥500,000, and she's responsible. The headhunter also
offers to pay off 60% of her debt if she'll come to Club A. This is where
a girl gets a chance to negotiate. Sometimes they go, sometimes they
don't, but this is one technique. It's better for a girl to go with someone's
help, especially if her current club is *yakuza* connected. If she has
someone from Club A doing the talking for her, it makes things easier
because she can't change clubs without everyone knowing about it.
People know when a girl changes clubs from Kyoto to Hokkaido [an
island in Japan's far north], so they're sure to know when she changes
clubs right in Kyoto.

"Long ago *yakuza* were involved only in gambling. They controlled
horse races and the like. As times changed and *yakuza* were able to
earn bigger profits, they expanded their range of activities, so now there
are some high-class clubs directly owned by *yakuza*. Again, the public
doesn't know this, or no one would come. It's the same thing in
America. If you have a place that everyone knows is Mafia-run, who's
going to go?

"The Mafia in America is into the drug trade, while *yakuza* in Japan
are more into other things, but it's all the same story, the world over.
The conditions of a particular country at a particular time may make
crimes different in form, but the end results are the same. By the same
token, even within Japan itself there are differences in the form crime
takes. Gion being as old as it is, it appears that there are places such as
geisha teahouses where *yakuza* have absolutely no influence. The
more than fifty percent of Gion bars connected with *yakuza* is also
gradually decreasing. Police controls have been getting tougher lately.
Even so, there are many things the police can't control, like the trading
of girls from bar to bar."

Mr. S. explains some of the background that helped make *yakuza* what they are today. "Until Japan was defeated in World War II, *yakuza* were in such poor shape financially that they'd almost disappeared. It wasn't until after the war ended that they regained strength and made their comeback. Until then Korea and Taiwan had been Japanese colonies; Japan had to give up these countries because we were under a new set of laws, the laws America set up. We were the bad guys; we were defeated. No matter how despicably we were treated, if we were insulted, spit at or kicked, we had no choice but to shut up and take it. The Taiwanese and Koreans were in a position to get back at us, and there was nothing Japanese police or officials could do about it. It was the *yakuza*, some of the guys from the army, who stood up for people's rights.

"Today's *yakuza* are bad, but in the old days, they were the ones who stood up for the weak in the face of abuse from the powerful. *Giri* and *ninjoo*, duty and compassion, that's what the original *yakuza*, known as *kyokaku*, represented. Do you know who Kunisada Chuji is? He started the *yakuza*, and he was a fine man. He opposed the government when they tried to impose unfair taxes on the people. It was around the turn of the century that things changed. Until then men like that would have died for justice, for their country. People with that kind of spirit are gone. There isn't one in a hundred today. So when you say the word *yakuza*, you're talking about a wide range of people, from truly good men to the lowest of the low. Why have the *yakuza* gone bad over the years? Because they've lost their sense of *jingi*, their moral code. In the American sense of the word, they've lost their pride. This applies not only to today's *yakuza*, it applies to all Japanese. The true Japanese spirit of the old days doesn't exist in even ten percent of the people today.

"Before the war, we predicted that the 'freedom' Americans had was something that would lead to corruption and decadence. Don't get me wrong—I think freedom itself is a wonderful thing. I also think the connection that Japan and the U.S. have now is good. Unfortunately, people don't understand the true meaning of freedom. There's a difference between freedom and pure self-indulgence. Having the right to do what one wants but maintaining a sense of right and wrong is real freedom. People don't understand that. Look at the problems you have in the U.S. The government gives out money to people who then do nothing but get drunk or high and go around committing crimes. We have the same problem in Japan.

"The *yakuza* of old were a group outside the government that kept society in order. That was their purpose, to help the people. The number-one rule, the symbol of what it meant to be a *yakuza*, was that a member never did anything that would cause trouble for non-*yakuza*. That spirit is gone now. There are set rules within the *yakuza*, and when a man joins, he agrees to those rules. But it's like traffic laws: When the speed limit is forty, people are driving fifty and sixty. It's the same thing with *yakuza*: Some men are determined to be good *yakuza*, like the *kyokaku* of old, but they find out it's a tough world, that surviving reality is hard, and things change. One rule gets broken, and then another. Somebody knows inside that what he's doing is bad, but if he wants something badly enough, he'll do it anyway.

"Let's look at an important subject, the question of good and bad, right and wrong. What do you consider to be right and wrong? All the philosophers in the world can't come up with a definitive answer. What's right in America isn't necessarily right in Russia, is it? In a way, however, everyone has some sense of the same basic rights and wrongs. The problem isn't so much knowing the rules, it's following them. When there's money at issue, people break rules. Japan's *yakuza* and America's Mafia know what's right and wrong, but man was born with desires, ambitions, and a sense of territorialism. To achieve their goals men will kill, even though they know it's wrong.

"This brings us to a social issue. Let's look at war, for example. Japan has been labelled a war criminal because of aggression in Asia during World War II. I don't think we are war criminals any more than anyone else. Didn't Americans go in and take land from the Indians? China and Korea were attacking Japan long before we occupied them during the war. The one who loses gets the label of war criminal, but everyone was doing the same things. What a country did one hundred years ago wasn't bad, but if they did it ten years ago it is.

"What's right in Japan is different from what's right in another country. What's right in this house isn't the same as what's right in the house next door. There's no end to it. The rules are different every-where. The *mizu shobai* world's rules are different from other people's rules. Let's look at it another way. There's adultery in America, isn't there? Well, there is in Japan, too. It used to be that no wives ever committed adultery, but that's changing, too. Now, fooling around has become the hot thing for housewives to do. Adultery, premarital sex, anything goes.

"This is all the result of too much freedom. You don't find much of this happening in China, though; they're still at the stage Japan was before the war. Talk about lack of freedom; Chinese women can have only one child. It wasn't so many years ago when I visited China that men could get permission to marry only after they'd been in the army. What about men who can't serve in the army? Does that mean they can't get married? Get strict with people and they cry for freedom. Give them freedom and they go too far out of control. It's hard to find a balance between too much freedom and too little.

"Let's look back at the *mizu shobai*. The idea that women go into the business to help their families or because they have no choice is a thing of the past. Maybe one in a thousand women go in for those reasons now. Now most women choose to work in the *mizu shobai* because there's more money in it than in anything else for women. The new freedom women have has made it easy for them to sell their bodies; sex has become a woman's biggest asset. From the top-class clubs to the sleazy sex joints, it's all the same thing. They may look different from the outside, but the business is the same, the systems are just different. I'm not saying that every single bar hostess sleeps with customers. That's a matter of individual pride in oneself.

"You seem to believe that some women in the business aren't prostitutes. Let's just look at the question of what a prostitute is. The way I see it, any woman who marries for money—no matter what country she's from—is a prostitute. And taking alimony payments or having a quickie for money, the logic is the same. Doing it under the guise of propriety or doing it with a sleazy image, that's the only difference.

"Long ago, before the days of equality for men and women, women had to follow men's orders to have sex as if they were animals, like pigs. Nowadays women can choose whomever they want. No matter how much a man offers to pay, if a girl wants to say no, she can. Today, probably only ten percent of prostitution is forced. Eighty to ninety percent of the women in the *mizu shobai* now choose to use sex as a money source. It doesn't have to be for cash, it could be for clothes or the rent on an apartment."

Mr. S. started to talk about the sleazier sex operations. "The real low-class *yakuza* are connected with pink salons, date clubs, and telephone clubs. The girls there are low class, too. You must have some in America, too. You know, if it's sex, anything goes, anybody goes.

There are women who sell it for a million yen, and others who'll do it for ¥5,000. It's the same all over. It's embarrassing to admit, but nowadays at these telephone clubs there are high school students, college students, even junior high girls and housewives. It's just a little side job to them. People want more for less these days. They want to look good, so to buy the latest fashions they do this work. It's the fastest money maker they've got. Sex is profitable.

"Let's look at top-class corporations, for example. The women who work at large Japanese companies are the elite, from the good families of Japan. The image they portray is that they only date someone they intend to marry, but that's just an image today. Let's get down to basics. Are food, clothing, and shelter really all there is? After eating and sleeping, what desires do humans have left? Women, men, we're all the same. Does everyone wait until they get married? If you're hungry, don't you eat?

"The girls at these top-level companies want it and so does a man, so why not? Especially if it improves their lot in the company. My friend, an executive at Sony, tells me stories. Women who play up to their boss can work in the section they want and the boss treats them well. Nothing but merit comes of it for the girl, so she thinks. She doesn't even actually have to have sex, she can just spend time with him, go out for dinner, provide pleasant company. It's the same basic thing. The only difference with girls like that and girls in bars is the class level. Some girls get their benefits by being friendly to the president, others by warming up to a low-level guy." Mr. S. laughs, "Let's face it, after dinner, sex is the only thing left to do at night!

"How will things go from here in terms of the *mizu shobai* and the *yakuza*? Things are going to get worse and worse in Japan. We're following just behind America; we're heading in the same direction. Laws are too light, too easy on people; it's time to make them tougher.

We don't have any real politicians in Japan now. There's no one out there who really stands up for what is right. If Japan had a war today, even with a lot of weapons, we'd lose in an instant. The people of Japan used to be like the Vietnamese: They were ready to die for their country. We were like Iran and Iraq are today. If you died, you'd will yourself to be reborn and fight again for the cause. Someone with that spirit in him is strong in battle.

"I'm not saying that wild, barbaric killers are strong, I'm saying that people who really believe in something are. Now the only thing people think about is money. Japan wasn't like this right after the war, it's only been in the last twenty or thirty years. After the war everyone had to work together to overcome hardships and poverty. There was a group spirit."

What about the image of *yakuza* as wild men with missing fingers and tattooed torsos? "Sure, you've got the guys out there with their fingers missing, with tattoos, wearing flashy clothes, gold and permed hair. That's what the weak guys do. A real *yakuza*, a man with power, is someone you'd never know was a *yakuza* by looking at him. The finger cutting is real. It's a form of apology. If a guy screws up the finances gambling and gets behind with some money, he has until the next morning to come up with it. If he can't get the money, he cuts off a finger segment in penance. It doesn't happen as often as it used to, but it still goes on. There are people with no fingers left. They've had to do it ten, twenty times. Usually a guy can cut the piece of finger, wrap it up in a cloth, and take it to present to the boss, but sometimes guys have to do it right there in front of everyone. I know a guy on Shijo Street who barely has his hands left.

"It's the same with tattoos. Many guys do it because they want to, but there are cases when they are told to, because the tattoo is the symbol of a real *yakuza*. Sometimes there are signs at saunas saying 'No *yakuza*,' but no one can be turned down at the public bath; everyone is free to go. Even if a public bath manager sees a guy with a tattoo and wants to send him away, what is he going to say? Having a sign out like that is a matter of form; a shop can put that sign out to keep up its own image and still have *yakuza* inside. No one knows who's inside, and it doesn't matter, as long as the place is keeping up appearances.

"When *yakuza* kill, it usually doesn't have much to do with the *mizu shobai*, unless it's a matter of someone stepping into another group's territory. Most killings are a matter of saving face. One group does something that humiliates another, and they have to make up for it. This recent business of guys going into hospitals as if to visit someone and then killing a rival gang member right there in his hospital bed with other people around—this is no good.

"Today's *yakuza* don't follow the rule of not bothering other people. The Yamaguchi Gumi [Japan's largest gang] has been doing some bad things. We shouldn't have these cases where bullets go through the windows of everyday families' homes. That's no good. One of the basic rules of old for *yakuza* is that we don't kill anyone outside of the *yakuza*. If a guy did that, he'd be expelled from the group. It's just recently that we have such stupid guys in the *yakuza*. A lot of the killing is just over territorial fights. It's the same with any war or fight around the world."

Mr. S. says there isn't much connection between *yakuza* killings and the *mizu shobai*, but what about the dangers the *japayuki-san* face? "The *japayuki-san* issue isn't something the Japanese *yakuza* started. People from those third-world countries see an opportunity to make a lot of money in Japan, many times more money than they could make in their own country. It's like the California gold rush—people see a chance and they go for it. The Philippines has its own version of the Mafia, and they've joined forces with Japan's *yakuza* to run that business. These are the low-class *yakuza* we're talking about. The guys doing that are from the *tekiya* class, the low-ranking guys who are usually running little shops or food stalls. Japanese women are expensive these days, that's why they're importing these women from poorer countries."

What percent of all of the *yakuza*'s activities involves the *mizu shobai?* "Somewhere between ten and twenty percent, I'd say. All of the men who are *yakuza* have to pay money to the guy at the top. It's similar to the Edo period, when the feudal lords had to make annual visits to pay homage to the shogun. One guy makes his money from prostitution, another from drugs. Some other guy makes his from gambling while another is a *sookaiya*, disrupting stockholders' meetings. Everybody has to make money somehow.

"The biggest yakuza income has to come from gambling. Look at Sasakawa Ryoichi. There's a man who used his head. After the war, when Japan was in trouble financially, the government gave him permission to run his motorboat races as a means of creating income. It's non-taxable, like a religion, because he had permission to run it as a nonprofit organization. Sasakawa clung to the permission the government gave him and has been making money ever since, and they can't stop him. When yakuza want money, they can't very well go to the bank and ask for a loan, so they go to Sasakawa. He's his own loan company.

"Real estate deals and gambling are the big money makers for the *yakuza*; they probably make up two-thirds of it. The rest is probably bars and *sookaiya*. Prostitution and things like that are done by *chimpira*, the young punks who aren't true *yakuza*. The real bosses, the real organizations don't run those deals. It's not that they don't know it exists, but it's the same with the Mafia, the big guys at the top pretend not to see all that petty stuff at the bottom."

I ask Mr. S. if *yakuza* are spreading to the United States. "You hear stories about Japanese gangster influence increasing in Hawaii, the West Coast, and major cities in the U.S. It's not just *yakuza* acting directly. Let's say big conglomerates like Mitsui or Mitsubishi want to make some kind of a deal in the United States, say they want to buy something like land, a building, or company. They make things easier for themselves by getting the *yakuza* to do the negotiating for them. It's like having a guard system. There's no way to prove that, but it's a pretty sure guess that it happens. It's not simply a matter of their presence being a threat. There are many ways to use the *yakuza* to achieve a goal. Say one of these companies wants to buy some land in Hawaii. They use the *yakuza* to check out the situation, and perhaps to cause people to want to sell their land and houses. It makes things easier for them.

"It's like war. If you can't get in from the front, go from the rear. If you can't get in from this side, go from the other. It's a matter of strategy. It's not that the *yakuza* are trying to cause trouble, they're just being used by someone else who wants something. There have been a lot of bad feelings about land being bought by Japanese in Hawaii, but in a way, it seems like a natural progression. There's not much anyone can do. It's not just happening in Hawaii, it's happening to people in Japan, too. When someone with money wants to buy something, they usually find a way."

Mr. S. criticizes American influence on crime in Japan. "Having all these guns all over the world is something you can blame on America. America's a country where someone can order a gun by sending in a postcard. That's a system that the government allows. Probably eighty percent of the guns gangsters of the world use are from America, most of them old weapons from the U.S. military. Did you know that at one time Japanese police were using guns that were originally used for shooting horses in America?

"Do you know what *yakuza* means? It means 'no good,' literally '8,9,3,' the worst roll you can get in a gambling game. There are excellent men at the top, but the guys at the bottom don't listen. You want to do something clean and nice and make money? Forget it. Being good doesn't make big money. All of Japan's *zaibatsu*, the big financial groups, are doing bad things. There's nobody who's only done good who's created a *zaibatsu*.

"That's why my wife didn't make a profit in her club. She was too nice. She was nice to her girls, and she didn't charge high prices. Her father died, and she had to quit school to work. She met me and I found out that her dream was to be the mama of her own club, so I set her up in her own place. She didn't have to make a profit, because I was behind her and she was running the place because she liked it. Her place had a kind of a homey atmosphere.

"She ran the place for ten years, and quit fifteen years ago. Most of her business came from men that were specifically her customers, not her hostesses'. Her girls didn't have many customers of their own, and that's part of the reason that she could stay in business for as long as she did. There was no reason for anyone to try to pull any of her girls to another club, because they didn't have a customer following. In those days you couldn't just be pretty, you had to be educated and sophisticated. Nowadays the girls are the pits. Back then you couldn't get by just by selling your body. My wife's girls didn't sleep with customers for money. That doesn't mean they never slept with anyone, it means that they only went to bed with guys they really liked, that they had something special with. The problem today is that there aren't enough girls. There are lots of new bars going up and not enough girls to go around. There are so many places open now that they can't keep busy, but they need girls to get customers.

"The *mizu shobai* people back then couldn't charge the high prices of today even if they wanted to. People back then were poor, no one would have been able to pay. Then the prices were low, the service was good, and the women had pride in themselves. Nowadays as long as there are girls and a place to sit, a place can open. Service doesn't matter, it's awful. The rents are a lot higher than they were back then of course, so the prices have had to go up. Thirty years ago a girl's monthly pay from a bar could be ¥15,000, whereas now it's more than ten times that. In those days you could buy a club in Gion for ¥500,000, and now it's ¥20,000,000.

"I've been to America. I went to see what the bars were like there—you know, the places where the girls come out and dance topless on top of the bars. Can't say they were all beautiful, but . . . I was also taken to see porn flicks, and saw some of America's underworld from behind the scenes as well. I've seen a lot of things, but I have yet to bump into an American street gang, and I was never mugged. Don't you get scared with all those people carrying guns in America? At least here you know the only people with guns are the *yakuza*, and they keep them hidden and only use them on each other.

"It's good for girls at bars to have a *yakuza* boyfriend in some ways. If people know she has someone like that standing behind her, they won't give her a hard time. Prejudice against women of the *mizu shobai*? It barely exists anymore. Sure, it used to have an effect on whether a girl could marry or not, but not so much anymore. Men are weaker than they used to be. It used to be that men chose the women they wanted to marry, now the women are choosing the men. Some people feel bad for girls because they're in the bar business, but then again, if a girl loses her job at a bar for some reason, *mizu shobai* people would feel sorry for her. It's all a matter of perspective."

My interview with Mr. S. left me both charmed and curious. After spending hours with him and his wife, both of whom were very down to earth, warm and friendly, I regretted that I hadn't met them earlier in my stay in Japan. I imagined them as a sort of friendly aunt and uncle far away from home. While this feeling of closeness and ease was quite strong, at the same time I felt a sense of awe at what this man represented. He was obviously quite knowledgeable about many things, not just in Japan, but in the world. His comments on world affairs, not all of which could be included here, showed a perspicacity and interest in international goings-on not often seen in many Japanese—or Americans, for that matter.

Mr. S. exuded a sense of control and confidence that made me wonder just how completely retired he was. His role had obviously been one of fairly high rank; one did not have his lifestyle in Japan without a great deal of power or a massive inheritance. He spoke of many things, he charmed, he convinced, but he never told his own story. That is perhaps why he'd survived as far as he had. Retired in comfort and wealth, he had known when to speak and when to keep quiet not only with me, but probably throughout his career.

The romantic heroism he speaks of in the *yakuza* of old may be just that, pure romance. Many a tale has been told of Robin Hood-like characters who stood up for the downtrodden in Japan's feudal period.

The *yakuza* themselves still claim their ideals, many of them the same ideals of the glorious samurai tradition, to be of noble origin and purpose. Why is it, then, that the *yakuza* of today are no good, that they are just punks out causing trouble instead of tragically honorable men performing heroic deeds? What happened to those good old days? Perhaps, as many of us realize upon close inspection of our own past, and that of our culture, the good old days weren't really so good after all.

MIZU SHOBAI,
PAST AND FUTURE

As this book nears its end, some may be curious about what actually caused me to quit hostessing completely. I started the job because of the unscrupulous practices of one language school, and I quit because of the same problems with another. Since I was working as a language teacher during the day, I was concerned that my nighttime occupation would be discovered by my school staff or my students. Since clubs are centers for business meetings between large companies, I often imagined fearfully that some day one of my own businessman students was going to walk through the club door and discover my secret. I never really thought of what would happen beyond that point, how I would explain what I was doing there or what might happen if my school found out, but I felt increasing anxiety about being discovered as time went on. Statistically, the longer I was there the more chance there was of being caught.

I also felt myself sliding into a pattern that many hostesses do. I was starting to hate men. Though I had good friendships and relationships with men outside of the club world, and I even liked some of the male club workers and customers, the overwhelming feeling I had every time a new set of customers came in was one of disgust and distrust. The mental conditioning of club life had affected me strongly in only a matter of months; I could only try to imagine what the women who had worked as hostesses for years must feel. In the back of my mind, I knew that it was not healthy to see the world through the eyes of a hostess for too long, yet I was becoming more accustomed to the job not only because it paid well, but also because my hostessing skills had improved enough that I could actually enjoy myself a good part of the time I was working. The thought of leaving the hostessing world completely left me with mixed feelings.

The Japanese receptionist at the language school where I taught started wondering why I was so dressed up on certain days. She was a friendly person, and seemed warm and understanding. I admitted to her that because I was given only half the teaching hours I had been promised by the school, I had to work as a hostess a few evenings a week to pay my rent and eat. When the news eventually got back to the American couple that ran the school, who knew the position they had put me in financially by lying on the contract about my working hours, they gave me an ultimatum. Either I quit working as a hostess, which my visa did not allow, or I quit working at their school. I was also expressly told not to tell the immigration authorities anything about their not living up to their terms of the contract.

Fortunately, it was the hiring season at language schools again, and I had been in the Kyoto-Osaka area long enough to have heard of more reputable schools than the two I had already worked at. I quit hostessing as well as teaching at that school, and went to a company where I not only taught but worked as a writer and editor, and later went on to be the editor of a small magazine in Kyoto. It was not long after I quit hostessing that I started doing research for this book. After many years of interviews and research, the book idea has become a reality.

I told many people that I was working on a book about the nightclub, sex, and entertainment industry in Japan, but very few knew that I had seen it firsthand. Those who did perhaps thought that I had started working at a club for the purpose of creating the book, rather than creating the book as a result of falling into the bar business. Fellow Westerners familiar with the difficulty of making ends meet in Japan and those who understood the taste for adventure and curiosity about the *mizu shobai* world knew that I worked as a hostess, but there are also many who did not.

Of the family and friends who have known about this book project, most will not realize that I actually worked as a hostess until they read these pages. Anxiety about having someone misunderstand or disapprove of my time spent pouring drinks, lighting cigarettes, and fending off advances in Japanese bars has stayed with me right up to finishing the book. As a manager at a branch of a large Japanese company here in the U.S., I have not spoken of this book or its subject matter to Japanese staff members, feeling that it would be truly difficult for them to comprehend all of the motives and background behind the project.

The group of people I have been most concerned about offending and causing problems for is my Japanese husband's family in Osaka. Oddly enough, my in-laws know about this book and my hostessing career, and they have not only taken an interest in my ideas about the sociological aspects of the *mizu shobai*, but have actually helped me gather information on related history and current events.

Spending time in Japan's *mizu shobai* influenced me in many ways. The strongest feeling I have about it all now is that entering that world, as so many others have before and will in the future, provided me with an education that I could have obtained nowhere else. I learned about business, history, and an inner culture that profoundly affects the larger culture in which it is embedded. And as we see from stories like that told by Kimi-chan below, this same inner culture is now affecting an even broader cultural base, the international business world. The *mizu shobai* is just one part of the many elements one must have knowledge about to have a true understanding of one of the world's major contemporary players, Japan.

The latest trend in international entertainment exchange is not surprising, given Japan's prominence as a worldwide economic power. Japanese now do business all over the world, and Japanese bars and clubs are appearing in various locations outside Japan. The United States is a major market for Japan, and a major location for business dealings, so it makes sense that the Japanese would build Japanese drinking establishments here so they can do business and relax in an atmosphere that's familiar to them. In the last ten years, the number of Japanese bars and clubs in the United States has mushroomed. The system of having girls as part of the club facilities is a somewhat foreign notion to many Americans, so the Japanese have imported their own women to act as hostesses at Japanese clubs on American turf. Kimi-chan, an art student on a college exchange program in San Francisco, talks about the bar business in San Francisco's Japantown as well as in America in general.

KIMI-CHAN

Kimi-chan was already familiar with the club world when she was a student in Japan. "I started working as a hostess in Osaka's Minami when I was eighteen. I told my parents I was a waitress, and they didn't say anything about it because I got off work at 11:00 at night, just as waitresses at a coffee shop or restaurant would. I quit that place after only a short time. I worked for eight months at the next place, where there were about fifteen girls. After that I changed clubs again and then worked at two places at the same time. I had to stay up late, but I made more money."

In all, Kimi-chan worked at half a dozen places or so in Japan when she was between eighteen and twenty. For someone who hadn't had time to build up a list of regular customers, Kimi-chan made quick jumps in income in her short career. "I made between ¥250,000 and ¥300,000 a month for working 7:00 to 11:00 six nights a week. I made ¥20,000 a day for working 8:00 to midnight at one place, but I had to spend a lot of money on clothes. The most I ever made was between ¥700,000 and ¥800,000 in a month, but just buying one handbag can cost ¥100,000, so the money goes quickly."

How do these businesses in America that are run by Japanese for Japanese get started? "Most of them aren't just single businesses. My place, for example, is owned by a guy who also owns and runs a couple of other restaurants and bars. His father had a lot of money and got it started for him, but he was smart enough to run it on his own. He left and there's a new guy in charge now, but if word gets around that the original guy is going to be in San Francisco even for just two or three days, all the big customers show up to see him." The "big customers" that Kimi-chan refers to are some of Japan's top-ranking businessmen in the U.S. on business. "We get high-ranking guys like the director of Toshiba and the head of Nagoya Meitetsu, as well as regular middle-class customers. There really isn't anywhere else for them to go."

After making so much money at such a young age, Kimi-chan found the situation in America to be very different. "The Japanese bars in America are much cheaper, both in the pay to the worker as well as the cost to the customers. Almost all the customers are Japanese. In Japan the customers often have a running tab, but here they almost all pay by credit card."

How does the atmosphere differ from the clubs in Japan? "It's completely different from working in Kita Shinchi or Gion. All of the girls are amateurs, for one thing. The clubs advertise in Japan, offering a job that girls can do while studying English in America. They bring the girls over, and put them up in a dormitory in Japantown. If they didn't do that, they wouldn't have any girls. The place I work has more girls than any other Japanese club in San Francisco; there are twelve or thirteen now, but we've had as many as twenty. There are only two of us who are college exchange students; it's illegal, so most girls don't want to try it. The clubs know that, but they do it anyway."

Kimi-chan says that tips and *shimeiryoo*, the tip for specifically being requested by a customer, help make up for the lower wages—she makes only $5 an hour—but there are some extra challenges to the job, too. "We get Chinese, Koreans, and Americans in the club as well as Japanese, so someone has to speak English. There are only three girls who speak English at our place; they can't speak that well, but can at least make it through a basic conversation. There's no mama at our club. We have the president, manager, and three waiters, all Japanese. We also have a singer and a pianist, but sometimes we switch to *karaoke*. On busy nights, the ten or eleven tables turn over three times.

One table holds four or five people. Saturdays are slower because all the men go golfing. A lot of guys come in and drink on Friday night and then go out golfing on Saturday."

Despite the lower pay, Kimi-chan likes working in the States. "When I was working at a club in Japan, I had to buy expensive clothes, have my hair done, watch out for underhanded customers, deal with middle-aged hostesses who were always complaining to me. The guys who come to the club here are younger, and they know how to enjoy themselves more than the customers in Japan. There are lot of guys who left Japan when they were twenty, came here, and started their own companies. They are much more independent and fun than the guys in their twenties in Japan who go to clubs because they are dragged there by their superiors. Here, I can also get away with wearing pants, and all of the other girls are nice because they are just everyday girls, not professionals. There's no mama bossing us around. Everyone has a good time. I work only a couple of nights a week here, and I make around $1,000 a month. It's nothing compared to the money I made in Japan, but working here is more like hanging out with friends. It's so much easier."

What does Kimi-chan do about men with wandering hands? "When there are customers who try to touch me, I always grab their hand and say, 'Let's hold hands,' and laugh. If I hold their hand they feel I'm paying attention to them, but I'm not letting them touch me. The customers here are usually really nice to the girls, because we all seem like the girl next door. There are a lot of twenty-one and twenty-two-year-olds; everyone is under twenty-five. Guys who are stationed here come in groups and ask many of the club girls to go to company outings, or invite some of us to go golfing and then take us out to eat later."

What about the women who work there? Are they all Japanese? "The other clubs in town have older women, Filipinas, or Koreans. Our place has all Japanese girls. Some of the women at those other clubs can speak Japanese, but not all of them, and not well. Most of the customers have to speak English at work all day, and they want to speak Japanese at night, so they like to come to a place where all the girls are Japanese. That's why our club is popular."

How much does it cost a man to come to a Japanese-style bar in America? "A guy can easily spend ¥30,000 for a couple of hours at the same kind of place in Japan, but here, if a guy has $100, he can spend the whole evening. The cost changes a little depending on how busy or slow things are, but it's much cheaper than in Japan. Our place charges $10 per girl for thirty minutes. Then there's a table charge. If a guy comes to the club alone for an hour and asks for me, for example, he pays a $10 table charge, $10 for each half hour of my time, $10 for *shimeiryoo*, and maybe $20 for snacks and drinks. That's about $60, and then there's a tip."

For Japanese, $60 plus a tip for an hour at a bar may seem really cheap, but it's expensive to most Americans. "San Francisco is really inexpensive, actually. It's much more expensive in New York, Los Angeles, and Hawaii. There are about ten Japanese clubs in San Francisco, but only five or six where they have girls. I worked at a place in New York for a short time when I first came to the States. It was much fancier, the girls dressed up more, and it was more expensive. Some of the girls at our place in San Francisco don't even wear makeup." What about the gangster connection? "You hear a lot about the prevalence of *yakuza* in Hawaii, but San Francisco doesn't seem to have much Japanese gangster influence. I hear about the Chinese Mafia some-times, but they never come into the club. There seems to be more *yakuza* activity in New York and Los Angeles."

Does Kimi-chan feel prejudice working in the *mizu shobai*? "I didn't feel anyone was prejudiced against me when I worked at clubs in Japan, but I was always at a good club. There may be people who still look down on *mizu shobai* workers, but at the very least it's a job for which you can't be ugly or stupid. If people have a problem with it, I figure *they* can go and try to earn ¥500,000 or ¥600,000 a month. Here in San Francisco the girls at the bars stand out more because there aren't that many bars. If I go shopping during the day, everyone recognizes me as working at that club. It's not a very big town, so everyone knows each other."

Are any of the Japanese hostesses here legally, or is this another *karayuki-san* issue in reverse, on a smaller scale? "The girls who were sent over through advertisements do actually go to their English schools. Girls who are here on three-month tourist visas don't have to bother with going to a language school. There are girls who stay beyond the three-month limit, but if they really want to stay and work, they usually get a student visa and go to school, or they go back to Japan once and get a new tourist visa. There are some girls who find boyfriends here and marry them, but it's usually a Japanese guy who's stationed here. There aren't many girls who have American boyfriends."

In a world where Japanese men and women work with other Japanese, eat with other Japanese, and drink and sing with other Japanese, it's not surprising that there isn't much dating between these Japanese and Americans. They probably don't have much time to meet Americans in a relaxed, social atmosphere, even though they live in America. This is probably also true for Japanese stationed in Europe, Southeast Asia, or any other place in the world. It is also frequently true with any group of nationals living outside of their own country, but it seems especially true for Japanese people, a characteristic that they often attribute in part to their long centuries as an isolated island country, making it more difficult for them to relate with others outside of their unique society.

It is this belief that has brought them to the point of having Japanese hostess bars in the major cities of the United States and the world, and that will probably have us seeing many more of these drinking establishments in the near future. What will be interesting to see is where the *mizu shobai* world, with its odd combination of historical and sociological currents and eccentric assortment of gimmicks and trends, will lead next.

Japan's *mizu shobai*, its "water trade," is a multi-faceted industry. It includes businesses that cater to the elite of the elite, supplying the most sophisticated, restrained form of entertainment imaginable, as well as businesses that deal in the crudest forms of quick sexual gratification. The players on the *mizu shobai* stage reflect a bizarre mixture of humanity, including top company executives, power-wielding gangsters, ranking politicians, Buddhist monks, preservers of ancient tradition, curious Westerners, third-world economic refugees, desperate women, and lonely men. The list could go on and on, but perhaps the most commonly found participants in the working end of today's *mizu shobai* are independent-minded women and men seeking social and economic freedom in an often restrictive society.

The *mizu shobai* life represents a kind of freedom to many of those who choose the route of late-night drinking in smoke-filled rooms, sexual flirtation, and high pay. For the level-headed, intelligent person who chooses this path in Japan, it can truly provide a kind of economic and social freedom, but often and for many, especially the women who work in the more direct sexual-service businesses, it can become a self-imposed trap. Unlike the highly paid, non-prostitute bar hostesses, women who work in the soapland and pink salon sexual-service clubs often become addicted to the money they make, finding it difficult to change to a life that doesn't involve selling their bodies. *Japayuki-san* and many Japanese women as well are in a trap of a different sort, a real prison of locked doors, beatings, or drug-induced stupors that prevent them from escaping a life of cheap prostitution. This kind of sexual slavery is more often than not imposed by organized crime groups, but not always.

The stories of the many people represented here as part of the *mizu shobai* convey a wide variety of feelings and attitudes. Though many are evoked by the peculiar circumstances of Japan and its entertainment trade, none are completely unique to Japan. The people working in the *mizu shobai* are in many ways not so different from the rest of us. While circumstance and opportunity vary in different times and places, human motivation remains essentially the same.

Any shift away from women working in Japan's entertainment trade in the future will likely be the result of circumstantial changes rather than feminist ideals. Though there are Japanese women and men who talk and write about social issues including the degradation of those working in the *mizu shobai*, the business does not seem to be fading. The tables may turn to some degree in the not too distant future, however. Newspapers and other periodicals are increasingly running stories on a labor shortage in Japan due to low population growth, placing women in increasing demand in the regular labor force.

Many of today's brightest mamas may very well have taken the path of corporate executive had demand in the workplace opened that door for them. Despite omens that circumstances may change, as long as Japanese businessmen need an atmospheric place to seal their deals

and as long as there is such a thing as sexual attraction, the night
butterflies of Japan's *mizu shobai* are sure to thrive.

GLOSSARY

aijin banku Mistress introduction service

akasen Japan's legal red-light districts, which were regulated by the government and closed in 1958

aru saro *arubaito* (from German *arbeit,* "part-time job") salons, a lower-ranking type of bar in which women sat in booths with men who were charged by time as well as by alcohol and food consumption

beppin-san Local Kansai dialect for "pretty girl"

-chan Suffix added to names showing affection, less formal than the more common *-san*

chiifu "Chief," usually refers to the man in charge of ordering and preparing food and drinks in clubs

chimpira Young punk gangsters, low-ranking *yakuza*

danna-san Literally "master," refers to husbands or patrons of geisha

doohan System by which hostesses bring customers in as part of a weekly or monthly quota

Edo period Approximately 1600 to 1867, a period during which Japan was largely closed to the outside world

erigae Literally "collar change," the change of the under-kimono collar, symbolizing graduation from *maiko* to geisha

fugu Blowfish, famous for the deadly poison it holds as well as for its delicious taste

gaijin Literally "outside person," foreigner, more often than not used to refer to white Westerners

gei nashi no geisha Geisha without an art, thinly disguised prostitute

gei An art

geiko Affectionate local Kyoto term for geisha

giri A sense of obligation and duty

guramaa gyaaru Glamor girl

hanamachi Literally "flower town," geisha districts

Heian period From 794 to 1185, when Kyoto was the capital and cultural center

hote toru Hotel Turkish baths, hotel rooms used for prostitution with the flavor of Turkish baths, often without the bath service

ianfu "Comfort girls," women who comforted soldiers with sexual services

ichigensan okotowari Literally "first timers are refused"

irasshaimase Greeting of welcome

iromachi Literally "color town," sex district

japayuki-san Women from poor countries who go to Japan to work in the entertainment industry

jingi A term often used by the early, more heroic Japanese gang members, referring to their moral code

karaoke Literally, "empty orchestra," background music provided for customers to sing along to *karayuki-san* The name given to the tens of thousands of women who left Japan at the end of the nineteenth century to become prostitutes in Southeast Asia. *Kara* is a reference to China, and *yuki* means "to go."

kayookyoku Folk songs

kissaten Coffee shop

kompanion Companion, young woman hired to be a warm body at parties, not expected to have the artistic skills of a geisha or even the conversational skills of a professional hostess

kyaba kura Cabaret club, similar to hostess clubs, but usually using younger, more amateur women who perform on stage as well as serve drinks

kyokaku Literally "a knight of the town," *yakuza* word meaning a man of chivalry

libe-chan Liberal girls, scantily clad dancers who also poured drinks during the post-war period

Lolikon From "Lolita complex," refers to older men obsessed with young girls, frequently mentioned in discussions of Japanese sexual hangups

maiko Literally "dancing girl," young apprentice geisha

mama-san Top-ranking woman at a bar or club, often the owner

Meiji period Period of the Meiji emperor, from 1868 to 1911

migi ude Literally "right hand," number- two man

Miyako Odori, Kamogawa Odori, and **Kyoo Odori** *Odori* meaning "dance," these are three of the famous seasonal district geisha dances held in Kyoto annually

mizu shobai Literally the "water trade," refers to entertainment-oriented businesses including bars, nightclubs, and restaurants that have an uncertain flow of customers

mizuage danna-san *Mizuage* refers to a geisha's first sexual experience. *Danna-san* literally means master, but most commonly refers to a husband.

211

In the geisha world, it is the man who becomes a geisha's formal patron, who sponsors her activities with money and also takes her on as a mistress

nagauta Traditional long, epic songs

ninjoo Sympathy for one's fellow man

noo pan kissa No-panty coffee shop

noo pan massa No-panty massage parlor

ochaya Teahouse where guests are entertained by geisha

ohanadai Literally "flower money," hourly fee charged for geisha or *maiko* entertainment

oiran High-class licensed courtesan

okaasan Literally "mother," the proprietress of an *okiya*

okami-san Geisha teahouse proprietress

okiya Office-residence of young *maiko* and *geiko*

onegaishimasu Literally "please" or "I have a favor to ask," used as a call in the *mizu shobai* for a hostess to go to the manager to be assigned to her next table

oniisan Literally "elder brother," used in general to mean young man

onsen geisha Hot spring geisha, usually of the non-artistic variety

pachinko Japanese pinball-like game played for money or prizes

pinkku saron From "pink salon," bars with darkened booths for sexual encounters, pink in Japanese being the equivalent of the Western idea of blue, as in "blue movie"

rakugo Traditional Japanese comic story

-san Suffix following a name, used to show respect

sansho wa kotsubu demo piriri to karai "A pepper is small, but packs a sharp punch," an old saying emphasizing that small people and things are not to be underestimated *sekuhara*　Abbreviation of "sexual harassment"

senryuu　A satirical poem

shachoo　President of a company

shakuhachi　A bamboo flute, slang for fellatio

Shamisen no heta wa, korobu ga joozu nari　Literally "Those who are bad at the *shamisen* become good at falling down," meaning that geisha with no art become good at sleeping with men

shamisen　A traditional Japanese stringed instrument

shasei sangyoo　Literally "ejaculation industry"

shimeiryoo　An amount of money paid by a customer for requesting the company of a specific hostess

Showa period　Imperial period from 1926 to 1989

shunga　Literally "spring pictures," erotic prints that are censored in Japan

sookaiya　Stockholder-extortionist, common in Japan

sopurando　A "soapland," bubblebath brothel that used to be known as *toruko*, short for Turkish bath

sunakku　"Snack" or small bar

tabi　Japanese socks with first toe separate from the others, worn with traditional clothing

Taisho period　Imperial period from 1912 to 1925

tanuki　Japanese raccoon dog, a popular figure in traditional Japanese stories and folk art

tayuu　Top-ranking courtesans who also boasted of talents in the arts, but had a different appearance and style from geisha

tekiya　Low-ranking gangsters who usually run small shops or food stalls

tengu　A folklore goblin, represented by a mask with a very long, phallic nose *toruko* Short for Turkish bath, long the name for Japanese prostitution bathhouses

wabi-sabi The spirit of refined, simple elegance with a hint of loneliness that pervades many elements of Japanese art and culture

yakuza Literally "8, 9, 3," the worst possible roll for gambling dice, and the popular name for Japan's organized gangsters

yaritebaba Older women who call passersby into their houses, acting as pimps for the younger women beside them

yuujo Literally "play women," prostitutes

yuukaku Composed of the two characters for "play" and "wall," walled enclosures where women were kept for sexual play, the entrances and exits to which were kept guarded

zoori Traditional sandals worn with kimono